GOLD

crystal lewis

GOLD

a devotional

THOMAS NELSON PUBLISHERS
Nashville

Published in Nashville, Tennessee, by Thomas Nelson, Inc., Publishers.

Unless otherwise noted, the Bible version used in this publication is the HOLY BIBLE: NEW INTERNATIONAL VERSION. Copyright © 1973, 1978, 1984 by International Bible Society. Used by permission of Zondervan Publishing House. All rights reserved.

Scripture quotations marked NKJV are from THE NEW KING JAMES VER-SION. Copyright © 1979, 1980, 1982, 1990, Thomas Nelson, Inc., Publishers.

Scripture quotations marked KJV are from THE KING JAMES VERSION.

All interior photos courtesy of Crystal Lewis and Metro One Records.

Library of Congress Cataloging-in-Publication Data

Lewis, Crystal.
    Gold : a devotional / Crystal Lewis.
      p.   cm.
    Includes texts of songs by Crystal Lewis and others from the album Gold.
    ISBN 0-7852-7470-7
    1. Devotional literature. 2. Contemporary Christian music—Texts.
3. Lewis, Crystal. I. Title.
BV4832.2.L47   1998
242—dc21

                          98-15699
                          CIP

Printed in the United States of America.

1 2 3 4 5 6 BVG 03 02 01 00 99 98

This book is dedicated to those whose courage in the face of adversity, struggle, and suffering has strengthened my heart. I truly believe that God will do unimaginable things for others through your lives. You're examples of His peace to me:

The Wimber Family

Debbie Wimber

The Lams Family

The Barretts

The Youngers

Mrs. Miera

The Family of Gloria Cleveland

And to those who have supported my work and ministry and continue to support it through Gold. *May God bless your ministry and your lives and all those you love. And may those around you see Christ through you.*

contents

O N E

a faith as pure as gold

T he wind is whirling outside my house. It is frenzied and ethereal, as if a legion of ghosts were trying to pry their way in. Yet it seems almost animal, too, as if a desperate pack of wolves were snapping and panting after a fresh scent.

This wind is loud. Demanding. Jarring both the rafters and my sense of well-being.

But I'm warm inside because of my faith in the roof and the walls and the nails holding my house together as firmly as they seem to be. And because of the little electric space heater my husband, Brian, brought me for days like this. Oh, now and again a breeze whispers through the ceiling vent so faintly it is easily ignored.

Faith.

What else do I have faith in? The chair I sit in. The pen I'm using. A Boeing 737, which weighs forty-eight tons soaking wet, but last week I trusted it to fly—and keep on flying.

My car. I strap my two children, Solomon (four) and Isabella (two), in their car seats, and I have faith that eight small brake pads (with a combined surface area about the size of the piece of paper I'm writing on) will stop the car before it glides into oncoming traffic, even though it weighs more than two tons.

I have faith in God—and the work His Son, my Lord and Savior Jesus Christ, did on the cross—and in God the Spirit who applies that saving work to my life.

But my faith is fragile.

When the bank account is low and I remember the upcoming payroll. Or when Solomon's temperature climbs to 104 degrees. Or when ticket or CD sales drop. That's when I'm sure that life as I know it is going to change for the worse. There are times I have greater faith that this pen won't ever run out of ink (and I *know* it will one day soon) than I do in God's promise never to leave me or forsake me. Sometimes I have greater faith in that forty-eight-ton hunk of iron flying me to Cleveland than I have in the God of creation providing for me and my family!

The album *Gold* and this book of the same name are about such faith. My faith, your faith.

Now it didn't start out that way. It began like all our other albums, with no particular effort to build around a theme. With the others we didn't come up with a title song and then write companion songs around it. We just wrote the words and music for each song as the Spirit moved us until we had twelve unique songs. And judging by the acceptance of our last few efforts, that method worked fine—for those albums.

So we started out the same way with *Gold*.

Did you ever get up one day and start doing things as you always do them—perhaps in a disorganized, slapdash way—then suddenly realize that everything fits together far more effectively than you deserve? And when the sun set, you saw how the Lord orchestrated the day for His purposes and enabled you to accomplish things for Him that didn't occur to you when the day began?

Gold was like that.

Almost from the beginning, this album headed in unexpected directions—God's directions. And when we had written the twelve songs, God's anthem rang out. All the songs came together around the theme of gold—tried by fire.

My brother-in-law, Chris Lizotte, wrote the title song, *Gold*. He had recorded it on one of his albums, so as you can imagine, I had heard the song many times. But when we began to select songs for this album, I heard it again and it touched me as never before.

It is a great song and the title is a great title—it conveys such power, such meaning for the Christian. But what really drew me to the song was its message. The title *Gold* came from Job 23:10, "But he knows the way that I take; / when he has tested me, I will come forth as gold."

I immediately saw so much substance crying out from that verse for today.

"He knows the way that I take . . ."

When Christianity is being ridiculed, when godly principles are held in contempt, when sex, sin, and violence seem to have gained an upper hand in so much of what we see every day—from kids' TV programming to the evening news—we know God is with us.

Job 23:10 means that we can seek His wisdom and comfort when life simply overwhelms us. The song *Gold* deals specifically with single parenthood. No matter how a person ends up there, few experiences in life are more exhausting. Think about being on duty twenty-four hours a day, being both mother and father, having no one with whom to discuss the tough issues like discipline and what to teach when. The buck not only stops at the single parent's feet, it tends to slam him or her in the shins. A single friend with a seven-year-old daughter says the hardest thing for her as a single parent is attending her daughter's Christmas programs at school and watching families enjoy the program together while she sits alone.

Whatever the trial, we go through it with Him.

"When he has tested me, I will come forth as gold." This really spoke to my heart.

Sarah is a dear friend of mine. We went through our first pregnancies at the same time. Her husband is a musician with whom we're often associated, so we've become pretty good friends. We gave each other baby showers, endured morning sickness together, watched our weight skyrocket, and wondered if we'd ever be attractive again—together.

After Solomon and Kimberly were born, we shared opinions about breast-feeding and spiraling temperatures. The kids had their first smiles about the same time, and they teethed at the same time. We discussed preschools and educational computer software as well as schooling options—public, private, and home-schooling on the road.

We weren't joined at the hip, but we were friends facing similar issues together.

But, as it turned out, not all our issues were common.

A month ago Kimberly was diagnosed with leukemia.

Faith. At times like this, it's all we have. No words or actions, no comforting phrases, nothing we can say or do matters much except faith: that whatever the trial, God will see us through it, and when the fire subsides, we will be as gold.

Not only is *Gold*'s anthem about faith and the precious metal that results, it's also about the struggle that takes us through the trials. Real struggles like the one Sarah, her husband, and little Kimberly will be going through. And the conflicts a single mother faces as she deals with the issues surrounding her. The struggle we all go through as Christians in a hostile world.

The Struggle of Prison Living

Nowhere is the struggle to be a Christian more severe than in prison. I am active in a small women's prison ministry, and although I haven't experienced what these women face daily, I can understand the battle. Satan is alive and well in our prisons, making his presence known in the violence, the drug use, the intimidation, the poisoning relationships.

It's hard enough if you go along with it all, or carve out your own niche, or simply hunker down and survive. But if you've been touched by the hand of God, if you've given your heart and soul to the Lord Jesus, you're called to minister there, to stand up and be counted no matter what the danger.

Candy is a slip of a woman, certainly not someone you'd pick to win any fights. After being in prison about a year, she came to know the Lord. Before that, she helped smuggle drugs to the prisoners. After she was saved, she had to refuse. When she had been beaten several times, the smugglers finally left her alone. The struggle of the faithful.

A struggle that lasts your whole life. The Lord tells us to take up our cross and follow Him. He tells us that our lives will be ones of difficulty and persecution. But He also tells us He loves us and that He will be right there with us. The thread running through this album and book is: God's faithfulness to the end, the very last breath.

Each chapter begins with a picture that represents my life (see Appendix for photo captions), a song from the album, and an explanation of why I wrote the song. And within each chapter is a section, "Verses Behind the Song," in which I share the Scriptures that led to the song.

So as you experience the songs we've assembled for you, do two things. First, enjoy them. Let them work together with your senses to give whatever gladness they can. Second, think about what's being said, and if the message is worthy, apply it to your life.

My hope is that each chapter will help strengthen your faith, help purify you as gold as it's being refined, and ease your struggle, so that when the music fades you'll be that much closer to your Savior.

two

why?

My thoughts they overwhelm me
My mind cannot contain
The pain that is within me
Why

I long for understanding
I live to know the peace
That comes with being sure
Of something

My eyes are blind to Your ways oh Lord
Yet I've seen You love and care so

I rest in Your knowing
Though I may not know
I take on Your strength
As though it were my own
Standing on the promises
Your word for me provides

I find therein the answer
To the question why

My complaint today is bitter
But sweet is your reply
My questioning still lingers though
Why

You know each road I travel down
My heart and Yours are one
I just don't see the good
In all this

My eyes are blind to Your ways oh Lord
Yet I've seen You love and care so

Through suffering and sorrow
Come peace beyond belief
For our present set of circumstances
Serve only to remind us
Of the gold
We can't yet see

—Lyrics by Crystal Lewis

ften an incident inspires me to write a song. Such was the case with "Why?" This situation occurred at a church in southern California where I sing several times a year. I've been there often enough to develop some friendships. One such relationship became very special in the last year or so.

Linda and Mike, a young couple in the Lord, met me backstage one Sunday before the service. Linda anxiously informed me that her mother was in the audience. Her mother was not a Christian but had recently expressed an openness to the "ideas of Christianity," and therefore to the contents of the upcoming service, including the words of my songs.

Linda explained, "My mom and dad are quite elderly, and Mike and I have been trying to get them to church for some time." Linda took a deep breath. "I know if you would just sing 'Amazing Grace' my mother would surely accept the Lord."

Well, I sang that beautiful hymn. And you can imagine my joy at watching Linda's mom rise from her seat and come forward. My faith was buoyed by her humble surrender to Jesus.

Linda stayed with her mom after the service while Mike and their three children came back to thank me for letting God use me in that way.

Several months later, when I was back at the same church, I saw Mike and Linda again. They told me Linda's mom had passed away, and they had played my rendition of "Amazing Grace" at her funeral. What a bittersweet situation, the sadness at the death of a loved one, and yet the joy of knowing she was safe in the arms of her Savior!

Linda and her mother were very close and although Linda knew her mother was in a far better place, her death left a void that seemed, for the time being anyway, to be a reservoir of pain. "If the Lord knew He was going to take her home, why did He allow me to be so emotionally dependent on her?" Linda asked.

The question was still lingering in her heart when only a few months later her husband, Mike, died of a heart attack. God's divine plan had once again visited a terrible loss upon Linda.

Even as I write this I have to keep myself from asking, "Why, Lord? It's not fair. What about their three little children now without a father? What about Linda who now must raise those children alone? What about Mike's love for You, Lord, and his love for Your Word? The fact that he served You, Lord, with all his heart? Doesn't that count?"

Absolutely! Mike *is* home in glory! You see, we can beg and plead with God to see it our way until we're breathless, but the fact is: our Father knows best. Psalm 18:30 says, "As for God, his way is perfect."

The second incident occurred when Brian and I were taking a few days off in Napa, California.

I express myself best in words and music, so soon after I'd heard about Mike, I wrote this song.

Verses Behind the Song

*In this you greatly rejoice, though now for a little while you may
have had to suffer grief in all kinds of trials. These have come
so that your faith—of greater worth than gold, which perishes
even though refined by fire—may be proved genuine and may
result in praise, glory and honor when Jesus Christ is revealed.*
(1 Peter 1:6–7)

Why do bad things happen to good people? I've heard
countless people, Christians and skeptics alike, ask this
question. Why does God allow children to suffer? Why do
car accidents involving drunk drivers seem to kill the innocent while the driver walks away unscathed? Why do so
many "accidental" teenage pregnancies occur when thou-
sands of married couples can't conceive? And why are there
1.5 million abortions every year and a two-year wait on
adoptions?

I don't claim to have answers to these questions, but I do
believe the Bible provides hope and understanding.

In 1 Peter 1:7, one reason for our trials is revealed to us:
"that your faith . . . may be proved genuine."

But when it comes down to the wire, to my real-life
disappointments and problems, what then? Will I be able
to recall what I know and apply it to my situation with
faith?

All Things Work Together for Good

The apostle Paul was no stranger to suffering. He was stoned by hostile crowds and left for dead in Lystra. He was imprisoned in Jerusalem and then sent to Rome—and on his way there his ship wrecked on the island of Malta. He lived under house arrest in Rome for two years while writing his letter to the Philippians, which many scholars say was written about the time Nero began making Christians into human torches to light his banquets. With that and every other trial that had befallen him as a backdrop, he told the early Christians:

I know what it is to be in need, and I know what it is to have plenty. I have learned the secret of being content in any and every situation, whether well fed or hungry, whether living in plenty or in want. I can do everything through him who gives me strength. (Phil. 4:12–13)

The words of one of my favorite old hymns, "It Is Well With My Soul," echo his testimony. They say, "Whatever my lot, thou hast taught me to say, 'It is well, it is well with my soul.'"[1]

God is so faithful to His promises. One of the most telling examples in my own life began about two years ago. A major record label approached Brian and me, asking me to sign a long-term contract. In this business—with so many ups and downs and opportunities to fail—this contract would have smoothed out the bumps and made life a lot easier. Of course we would have given up some things, like creative control, which could include changing lyrics and/or music. We decided the Lord hadn't brought us this far to even slightly alter our message. We didn't sign. And in the next two years our own label flourished. We now have other Christian artists recording for us, and we have kept our message as pure as we can make it.

I know only that God's promises have been fulfilled, every one of them, to this point in my life. And I expect I will be able to say the same as I am being called home to be with Him.

God said He provides for the sparrows and surely He will provide for us. But sometimes that provision is not what we expect.

Paul put that truth this way to the Christians at Rome: "And we know that all things work together for good to those who love God, to those who are the called according to His purpose" (Rom. 8:28 NKJV).

Haven't you found this to be true? Isn't it part of your witness? How God has brought about something good from something that at first looked bad, even catastrophic? But how can such a devastating event as Mike's death work together for good? We do know that some good came of it. At least in Mike's case, his boss and his boss's wife heard the gospel for the first time at Mike's funeral and are now regularly attending church.

Believe it or not, when I spoke with Linda after Mike died, this was one of the first things she mentioned. As we spoke, I was so humbled by her sweet willingness to accept God's decision to take Mike home if his death might mean spiritual life for another. What a special helping of grace our Lord is giving her. And what love Linda is showing for Mike's boss and his wife, something like the love Jesus showed me when He gave His life that I might live.

So, who am I to cherish the appointment Jesus kept on the cross for me, yet question God's other appointments? God is sovereign, and although we may not understand right away—maybe not until we behold the Savior with our own eyes—we can rest in the knowledge that He has His reasons. When we are troubled or overwhelmed we can fall, by faith, into His open hands, knowing those hands have been pierced for us on the cross.

THREE

remember who you are

My daddy always told me
That his mama always said
No matter what you become in this life
Whether big or small in the eyes of man
Remember who you are in the eyes of God

Remember who you are in Jesus
He sees you as His own
It pleases Him to know that you
Remember who you are in Jesus
It's His name you wear my child
Remember who you are

So I am giving you now
This legacy of love
The greatest gift that I can give you is to pray
That whether big or small in the eyes of man
You'd remember who you are in the eyes of God

There is a song living deep within your soul
As life goes on that song begins to grow
Until that day when the world will need to know
Who you are
Remember who you are

—Crystal Lewis

I grew up in southern California—Anaheim to be exact. My father pastored the Anaheim First Church of the Nazarene. My mother manned the music ministry. She sang, she played the piano, she played the organ, she directed the choir, she directed the musicals, and she organized the special music, which often included me! For seventeen years my life revolved in and around that place.

I learned many things from my parents, some of which they probably thought would never take hold. One thing I remember particularly well, a phrase I've already used on my kids, has stayed with me through the years. My dad used to say, "Remember who you are." It was as though he were saying, "Don't forget who you are committed to represent. Don't forget whose name you wear. Don't forget whose child you are. Don't forget to let Jesus shine through you in word and deed."

As I left the house on my way to school or to church or on dates—anywhere I went—that phrase hung over my head as if it were written inside a little bubble, like in the funnies.

When I was fourteen, fifteen, and sixteen, my typical response was defensive, probably because I knew I wasn't setting the example expected from a preacher's daughter. I found myself in several settings that I, as a Christian, should not have been in.

One that comes to mind would be comical if it weren't so serious. I was fourteen and wanted to go where I wanted to go and do what I wanted to do. Both of those things happened to involve a carnival that had set up in a local church parking lot. I was big on rides, but I was much bigger on just doing what the rest of my friends were doing. My dad said no. I mean *really* said no. He didn't like the friends I ran around with, and carnivals, no matter where they were, didn't appeal to him. "OK," I said, and promptly joined my friends at one of their houses and made plans to go anyway.

This particular friend's mother decided that we all needed drinks—in the alcoholic sense of the word. (Now you can see why my dad was a little nervous about these kids.) So we had some beer and wine. Well, I didn't have much meat on my bones and a little alcohol went a long way. So, eyes blurry, walking a bit unsteadily, we all went to the carnival.

Now Dad isn't all *that set* against carnivals. He actually thinks they're fine for kids whose parents are along. So he decided to take my younger sister.

I had just staggered off the Ferris wheel, eyes looking off in different directions, when he and I spotted each other. He was pretty cool about it just then. But when I got home . . .

Satan has the uncanny ability to make inappropriate behaviors seem not so bad. Subtle is his middle name. I certainly didn't think I had done much wrong—at the time. But looking back, I think my father showed remarkable restraint just allowing me to live. That's why it is imperative that we follow the direction given in Ephesians 6:11–13:

Put on the full armor of God so that you can take your stand against the devil's schemes. For our struggle is not against flesh and blood, but against the rulers, against the authorities, against the powers of this dark world and against the spiritual forces of evil in the heavenly realms. Therefore put on the full armor of God, so that when the day of evil comes, you may be able to stand your ground, and after you have done everything, to stand.

Life is our battle. This armor is our protection. Only with our minds and hearts constantly set on our Commander in Chief will the victory be ours.

The Eternal Victory

My father grew up in Louisville, Kentucky, where his father pastored the Broadway Church of the Nazarene.

His mother spent her daylight hours keeping my dad and his five brothers and sisters clean, clothed, and fed. The rest of the time she was on her knees, before the Lord, on their behalf.

Her favorite thing to tell them was: "I don't care whether or not you are successful here on earth as long as you make it to heaven." That was her prayer for her family: that they know God and live a life of glad surrender unto Him.

And pastors' kids aren't the only ones required to live up to biblical standards. Any man, woman, boy, or girl who wears the name of Christ is to live according to the example set for us by Jesus Himself. Currently some are wearing the WWJD (What would Jesus do?) bracelets, which were first introduced in 1996 by a Michigan youth group. Those four little words are the only standard any Christian needs.

There is no secular side to the Christian life. Jesus must be Lord *of* all or He is not Lord *at* all. All or nothing. Yes or no. Christ is head of every aspect of our lives. And He knows and cares about all of it—even the smallest detail, just as a parent cares about every aspect of a child's life.

I have every intention of teaching my children what my parents taught me: that no matter what the world says they should do or be, it is God whom we strive to please. Finally, that every day, everywhere, in every situation and under every circumstance—they must remember who they are!

Verses Behind the Song

Therefore come out from them
and be separate,
says the Lord.
Touch no unclean thing,
and I will receive you.
I will be a Father to you,
and you will be my sons and daughters,
says the Lord Almighty. (2 Cor. 6:17–18)

Not only did my father reflect his own judgment in what he taught me, but he faithfully reflected Scripture, like this passage from 2 Corinthians. As a pastor and a Christian example to his congregation, and really to the whole community, my father had to be the good and proper father even at something as seemingly harmless as a local carnival. He needed to be there with his children making sure all went well. He probably wanted me to go with him but I didn't give him the chance to say so.

I wish I had remembered who I was before I disobeyed my dad and went to that carnival with my friends.

God wants us to be *in* the world, spreading His message of life and truth and peace, without being *of* the world and adopting its "Do what feels good" philosophy. Since I have small children, my challenge is often explaining principles like this so a four-year-old will understand.

The Lord told the Israelites to teach their children well, to talk about Him all the time, to write His laws on their doorposts. Our job is to help our children clothe themselves in the full armor of God, garment by garment.

A Child Can Put on the Armor

In our home we supply a lot of Christian music for the kids—like the Psalty tapes and videos, Veggie Tales videos—anything they'll find enjoyable as they absorb Christian messages. Even Isabella, "nearly two," gets most (but not all) of it. She goes around the house singing, "Jesus loves me, *I don't know!*"

And we have another way to teach the Word to Solomon and Isabella. Ever since I can remember, my father has carried what he calls his *charge card:* a card with a Bible verse on it, which he changes every month. He now lives in the state of Washington, and every month when he sends a new card, we teach the verse to Solomon. Then, to show his papa that he knows it, we put that verse on our answering machine as part of our greeting. Solomon has so much fun doing this, he looks forward to getting his charge card every month.

Solomon's favorite verse is Hebrews 4:12 (simplified): *The Word of God is sharper than a two-edged sword.* And his favorite toy is a little plastic sword.

Solomon is never afraid of the dark. He's always been a

brave kid. But one night the darkness got the best of him and he voiced concern after he'd climbed into bed and the lights went out. We had been learning 2 Timothy 1:7: "God has not given us a spirit of fear" (NKJV). I said, "You know, your favorite verse is Hebrews 4:12."

"The Word of God is sharper than a two-edged sword, Mama?"

"Yes. And that means the Word of God is our weapon, like your plastic sword. And what are we learning this month?"

"God hasn't given us fear . . ."

"A spirit of fear."

"Right."

"So we can use the Word of God as a weapon against our fears."

His eyes sparkled. "Hey, that's neat—OK, good night, Mama."

And that was that. Off to sleep he went.

It doesn't work that easily all the time. But just once made all our teaching worthwhile.

As adults, we, too, need to hide the Word in our hearts, so we can constantly remember who we are: sons and daughters of Christ. Jesus said: "I will be a Father to you, and you will be my sons and daughters" (2 Cor. 6:18).

When I consider the fact that we are children of God, one thing that comes to mind is the relationship between the earthly parent and child, which, among other things, includes love, discipline, protection, and comfort. Another story from my rebellious youth included all four and a little discipline from the Lord as well.

Again I was fourteen (an interesting year for me). And again I wanted to go somewhere. But when I asked my dad if I could go, he said flatly, "No!" I was crushed. I saw no valid reason why I shouldn't be allowed to go. It wasn't to be a dangerous outing. A group of friends and I wanted to take the bus to the mall.

So yelling something back at him, tears flooding my eyes, I ran from the house and headed down the street. The kids had gathered at someone's house a mile or so away. I got there and was about to dry my tears and greet them when my dad drove up.

Now the last thing I wanted to do was to humble myself and get in that car. But I did. I knew I had been rebellious and I knew he was my dad and we loved each other in spite of how tough things were at the moment. But he didn't discipline me. Instead he drove me to the bus and let me off. Later when we talked about it, he said that he'd had second thoughts, that where I wanted to go was OK and that he should have let me go in the first place.

The Lord disciplined me, though, for being a brat and showed me that I should have obeyed my dad no matter what. When the group was about three miles from our destination, the bus broke down and we had to trudge the rest of the way on foot. My dad had loved me by caring about what I did. Although he didn't discipline me then, he had in the past, and I knew that he wouldn't hesitate to do it again should the need arise.

Let's remember who we are.

FOUR

dyer road

Walkin down Dyer Road
Thinking 'bout life and lovin' livin'
Happy to know what I know
Glad to lead the life that I've been given
Not to say I never get down
I have had my share of sheer frustration
Through it all I finally found
I've got a God that knows my situation

I know it'll be alright
I know it'll be alright

Walkin' down Dyer Road
I'm delighted to know God is watchin'
Givin' me just enough
Information to keep me in trusting
Sendin' me a sign now and then
Just to make sure that I'm still listening

Every single promise has been
True to every word
You bet I trust Him

It's alright
Although sometimes I wonder
Alright alright alright
If I believe it all
I do I've discovered

—Brian Ray and Crystal Lewis

yer Road is a minor thoroughfare in southern California that runs not far from my home, but it's a *major* thoroughfare to me. It played a special role in the avalanche of events that culminated in Brian and me getting married.

I need to preface this story with a warning: kids, don't do this!

Why? Because Brian and I are part of the perhaps two percent who made a marriage decision in these circumstances and it didn't end in disaster. The Lord was really with us, and maybe we've made it because even though we were young, we made an effort to seek Him during the process.

With the stories I've already told you about my mid-teens, you can imagine how my parents reacted when I came home at age sixteen and told them I was dating Brian, a twenty-two-year-old. Well, as the years progressed and it became obvious to my parents that my relationship with Brian wasn't going to easily dissolve, they sort of went with the flow. We'd been dating a while when Brian began working at a restaurant on Dyer Road.

The next real concern for my parents was when I announced: "I'm not going to college." No parent wants to hear that. But I didn't want to go. I felt there wasn't much I could learn there that I wasn't already learning "on the job." I'd already recorded my first album (at seventeen). Yet my parents persisted, so after the dust cleared, I decided to make them happy and go anyway. My resolve lasted a year before I decided to leave school and come back home. During that summer Brian asked me to marry him. I accepted. And he gave me a ring. Not a big ring, but a beautiful ring. I told my folks.

I was eighteen. They were less than thrilled, to say the least. "What about school? What about your age? You're too young. Neither of you has a stable job that provides stable income. No."

You might suppose that I just ran right out of there and married Brian anyway. But I didn't. I returned the ring, and Brian and I sought the Lord. We sought Him in prayer, in counseling with my parents (my pastor), another pastor, and a lot more prayer. Six months later Brian asked me to marry him again and I accepted again. I was nineteen, and this time my parents, although still very concerned, gave us their blessing.

And we knew God had given His blessing, as well.

The song "Dyer Road" was born from that faith.

Verses Behind the Song

Therefore I tell you, do not worry about your life, what you will eat or drink; or about your body, what you will wear. Is not life more important than food, and the body more important than clothes? (Matt. 6:25)

As mentioned before, I live in southern California. Beautiful sunny, ocean-breeze-caressed southern California. I've always lived here. Don't want to live anywhere else. Oh, there are times when I worry about "the big one"—usually during one of the little ones when the plates are a-rattlin' and the chandeliers are a-swayin'. But the weather more than balances out that scale. Yet one December day in 1997—not all that many months ago—the weather let us down. There's a song called "It Never Rains in California," which must have been written by someone who lives in Omaha; at any rate, the writer wasn't here that December.

A storm hit the area surrounding my home with a force not seen in years. It was approximately five in the morning when my husband was awakened by the unfamiliar sound of rushing water.

Brian went downstairs to find nearly three feet of water boiling through our hallway and pooling in the kitchen and living room. Searching for a way out for this newly forming lake, he splashed to the back door, and after struggling with it for a while, finally pried it open. As he hoped, the water spilled out. Unfortunately, it left behind a thick trail of mud and sludge on everything—the Christmas gifts I had meticulously wrapped only a few days earlier, our VCR, the couches, the table and chairs, the food in the lower kitchen cabinets, even the food in the lower half of the refrigerator.

All that paled when compared to the loss of irreplaceable, truly priceless family photos and home videos. Overwhelmed, I fell against a wall and wept. The tears came from deep emotions I'd never experienced before—mostly from an unfathomable sense of having been violated. And I wanted to lash out at my attacker, but there was no one to kick or scratch, no one to blame. Finally I stood ankle-deep in mud and slime, tears coming in torrents, my hands planted defiantly on my hips and my insides crying out: *Who is going to take responsibility for this?*

"But it wasn't my fault," Brian said.

"You mean I said that out loud?"

The cause was that it *does* rain in southern California and when it rains a lot, the storm drains get clogged and the water looks for houses to run through. Flooding in southern California? Who'd-a thought it?

In our case, the rain didn't have far to look. Our house is in a depression, so all the rain had to do was gather at the base of our driveway, which runs *up* to the street, build a wall of water several feet high against the garage door, find out that the storm drains were overloaded, and come crashing through the door leading into the house. A piece of cake for any flood.

And it was all a nightmare from which we couldn't wake up.

There was good news, however—a lot of good news. And it all stemmed from the fact that we have no bedrooms downstairs. My two children slept under their cozy covers, unaware of the danger until they heard the sirens and the noise of the firefighters rushing into the house. At which time my four-year-old, Solomon, came downstairs and stared wide-eyed at the damage. "What happened to my house?" he asked.

Everything was put into perspective at that moment. I cannot tell you the thrill I experienced just knowing they were alive and able to wonder! Even the things I thought to be priceless were still just *things*. God was using a tragedy to teach me the value of things temporal versus things eternal. The value of things man-made versus the value of things God-made.

He wants to teach us that in the long run, there is no real preservation or protection of our *stuff*. There is, however, long-term preservation and protection for our souls. Yes, we lost a ton of stuff in the "flood." No, insurance won't cover it (it's a long story).

God knows our needs, and His way of providing for them is far and away better than anything man could devise.

Yes, I have a God who knows my situation.

I know it'll be alright.

I know it'll be alright.

FIVE

not the same

I used to be mean
Couldn't care 'bout a thing
Livin' for me
And all of my needs
I was self-serving
Yet desperate and hurting
In need to be

Not the same
No no no yeah yeah yeah
Jesus has changed me
Not the same

Ooh, it's all for You
All that I am
All that I do
I've given in to
Life-giving truth

I've come to believe
I can be new

He took all my sin
Gave peace within
Took all my doubt
Assured me of Him
He's now why I live
My life is His

All that I was
And all that I wanted to be
All that has changed
For I am not the same anymore
All that I am
And all that I ever will be
He's now why I live

—Brian Ray and Crystal Lewis

*S*ongs are sometimes inspired by a number of events, which culminate in my inspiration. This was the case for "Not the Same."

The first incident occurred when I was in sixth grade, which would make me eleven. A girl in my class, Tiffany, made extra money by creating plaster letters, painting them, putting pins on the back of them and selling them at school. Everything in my life seemed to revolve around some guy, and at that time I liked a guy whose first name started with "B." I thought it would be neat to wear this "B" on my jacket, so I bought one of her letters.

A couple of days later she delivered it and I didn't like it. I'm not sure why—maybe I'd just changed my mind. While she stood there waiting for her money, I backed her into a corner and stomped on the letter until it lay smashed on the schoolyard pavement. Isn't that the meanest thing you've ever heard? Of course she burst into tears and ran off.

I knew immediately what a painful thing I had done, but I didn't apologize. I lived for years knowing I had hurt her. I mean *years*. All through high school and beyond— five years to be exact. As I prepared to go to my five-year high school reunion, I promised myself I would find Tiffany and apologize.

When I first got there I saw her, but I walked right by. Then after another half hour or so, our paths crossed again. Once more I did my best to avoid eye contact; however, conviction kicked in, and I turned to approach her. "Tiffany, remember that terribly mean thing I did to you in elementary school?" No response. "Well, I want you to know, I did a horrible thing, and I apologize from the bottom of my heart. I'm sorry," I said.

"Oh, don't worry about it. Don't give it another thought,"

she replied and walked away. But I didn't feel as though she had truly forgiven me.

Well, I went about living the rest of my life, until a little more than a year ago I received a letter from Tiffany. She was apologizing to *me*. She and her husband had attended what's known as the Harvest Crusade, a contemporary, large-scale Christian outreach. It's part rock concert and part old-fashioned tent revival where the gospel of Jesus Christ is presented clearly and those attending are offered an opportunity to respond.

Tiffany was writing to let me know she'd heard me sing there and had become a Christian. She wanted to apologize for not accepting my apology those many years before. At it turned out, neither one of us was the same as before. I believe I was a Christian then, but not acting like one, and she was now a Christian and acting very much like it.

The second incident that inspired "Not the Same" occurred at my ten-year reunion.

A Significant Ten-Year Reunion

Interesting events, reunions. Half of the people look exactly the same. The others are unrecognizable.

And everyone has a different reason for coming. Some are socially dulled by the nine-to-five workplace and want to feel popular again. They're ready to rev up their old charisma and be who they used to be. Some, unnoticed the first time through, come to give it a second shot. Some, having been academic giants and social lightweights, come to see if there's any hope for them ever to command the spotlight. Still others, like me, come just to reminisce. For us the conversation usually begins, "What's been going on the last ten years?" and goes on to cover the good times, the bad times, and all the shades of gray in between.

It was all enjoyable and pretty normal until about two hours into it when I was approached by a young man whose face was vaguely familiar. He was nice-looking, clean-cut, well-dressed, and quite polite. He asked if I remembered him—and I drew a blank. He proceeded to tell me his name: Sammy.

Somewhat stunned, I immediately remembered him as having been in my math class (my worst subject). He sat in front of me and had always kept to himself, which made him seem smart. I remembered him with unkempt long hair and as having frequently worn a hooded gray sweatshirt with jeans and athletic shoes. Not much of a memory for having shared a space of about nine square feet an hour a day for almost a year.

He proceeded to tell me more: "Crystal, I've been looking forward to the reunion, hoping you were going to be here.

"I got saved! I knew that you were a Christian and I just couldn't wait to tell you!"

I stood silent, my smile coming alive.

"I don't know how much you knew about my life in school," he said, "but I came from a broken home. I was into drugs throughout high school. I just didn't care about life."

I began to see the high school Sammy very differently. (I wish I had known.)

". . . but I met Jesus, and I'm changed, I'm different."

A flood of memories with Sammy in them rushed back and, frankly, a totally different guy was standing before me. It wasn't just the obvious changes in his appearance, but the difference in his attitude, his demeanor, his mannerisms, and his facial expressions.

Then he told me about his church and his work in a ministry that involved underprivileged young people. He spoke with such enthusiasm and zeal.

We chatted a few minutes more and then went our separate ways, mingling with other classmates in the crowded room. Later, as I stood alone, I looked around that room. I watched as classmates danced to the same eighties music we had enjoyed just ten years prior. I watched as some sat and carried on conversations, seeming to have picked up right where they left off on graduation day. I wondered how many had experienced the same transformation as Sammy. I wondered which ones had been exposed to the light and which ones were still clambering around in the dark, searching for the way out.

There was no question Sammy had found the way. In fact, as I heard him witnessing to a classmate later, I could see he'd not only found his way out, but he'd hiked his way back to throw a lifeline to someone else. Their conversation had undoubtedly begun with that simple question: "What's been going on the last ten years?"

These thoughts about Sammy, about Tiffany and how our lives had intersected over the years were finally brought together in "Not the Same."

Verses Behind the Song

Therefore, if anyone is in Christ, he is a new creation; the old has gone, the new has come! (2 Cor. 5:17)

The change that took place in my classmates Tiffany and Sammy has occurred over and over again throughout the centuries and is recorded many times in the Bible. My favorite example is the conversion of Saul on the road to Damascus, since it is a graphic and vivid view of God's ability to work wonders. Paul told his story in Acts. Just picture him standing up in your church, admitting to these sins:

I persecuted the followers of this Way to their death, arresting both men and women and throwing them into prison, as also the high priest and all the Council can testify. I even obtained letters

from them to their brothers in Damascus, and went there to bring
these people as prisoners to Jerusalem to be punished. (22:4–5)

I don't know what Sammy did during his years of drug
addiction, but we can imagine. Yet think of what Paul did,
according to his own testimony. And then picture him telling
his story as you sit there in church. This must have been
how people in synagogues and Christian churches throughout the Roman empire felt as Paul gave his testimony.

But Paul's story didn't end there. He went on to say:

About noon as I came near Damascus, suddenly a bright light
from heaven flashed around me. I fell to the ground and heard
a voice say to me, "Saul! Saul! Why do you persecute me?"

"Who are you, Lord?" I asked.

"I am Jesus of Nazareth, whom you are persecuting," he
replied. My companions saw the light, but they did not under-
stand the voice of him who was speaking to me.

"What shall I do, Lord?" I asked.

"Get up," the Lord said, "and go into Damascus. There you
will be told all that you have been assigned to do." My com-
panions led me by the hand into Damascus, because the bril-
liance of the light had blinded me.

A man named Ananias came to see me. He was a devout
observer of the law and highly respected by all the Jews living
there. He stood beside me and said, "Brother Saul, receive

your sight!" And at that very moment I was able to see him.
(22:6–13)

Just imagine how Ananias and the other Christians felt.
Paul had killed their brothers and sisters in Christ. Yet Jesus
had forgiven him. Because of Jesus' death on the cross,
because of the blood He shed on our behalf, because He rose
again, we can be forgiven! Whatever Paul or Sammy did in
the past—when Paul persecuted Christians or Sammy got
high on drugs—has been completely washed away in God's
eyes. They are made new.

Most of us have not wasted our lives on drugs or alcohol
nor have we killed anyone, but we have all hurt friends and
loved ones with harsh words or actions. We all need to be
born again, saved, washed in the blood. However you word
it, it means the same thing: we must meet Jesus personally,
repent, and let Him change us, just like Paul and Sammy.
We must surrender our lives completely, purposefully, and
without reservation to His will. He created us; He could've
taken residence in us to begin with, but He gave us a choice.
And once we accept Him as Savior, we are new creations.

New Creations

Paul told the early Christians in Corinth: "Therefore, if
anyone is in Christ, he is a new creation; the old has gone,
the new has come!" (2 Cor. 5:17).

What does it mean to be a new creation?

Remember when my dad didn't want me to go with all those kids on the bus back in Chapter 3? This was a time that drove my mother, God bless her, truly nuts. I needed, absolutely needed (the same need I had for air and big bags of Fun-yuns), to be part of this crowd, so I dressed in vintage store clothes. The colors were old and faded, they were ill-fitting—and believe me, her cute little girl looked anything but cute in those clothes. Can you imagine what a pastor's wife, a woman who was trying to set an example as a godly homemaker, must have gone through every morning when her teenage daughter left the house on her way to who knew where looking like that?

Less than six months later I looked at myself in the mirror and agreed with her. What was I thinking? How could I have wanted to dress like that, let alone defy my parents? I immediately got back more closely in line with what my parents wanted for me.

Put that story on a spiritual level—make the old clothes our sins and our desire to do things that offend our heavenly Father—and that's what being a new creation means. It's looking at yourself spiritually in a mirror, and through the work of the Holy Spirit, throwing off the old and putting on the new: something far more fitting, far more representative of what our heavenly Father desires for us.

The analogy of my friends and me with the funny clothes

isn't completely accurate though. I didn't die to those people. I still spoke to them occasionally. But spiritually, we do die to our old selves: old things *do* pass away. Death is involved in becoming a Christian. The death of the old self (a change that is the same today in Sammy's life and my life and your life).

After putting to death the old self, we are new! Now we are able to begin the learning process. It is not as though once we accept Christ into our hearts God snaps His fingers and we are mightily and miraculously changed. Yes, we are mightily and miraculously forgiven, but the change—at least 100 percent of the change—doesn't happen with the wave of a wand. It is a growth process.

Right after Ananias healed Paul's blindness, he gave Paul this message from the Lord:

The God of our fathers has chosen you to know his will and to see the Righteous One and to hear words from his mouth. You will be his witness to all men of what you have seen and heard. And now what are you waiting for? Get up, be baptized and wash your sins away, calling on his name. (Acts 22:14–16)

The Lord transformed Paul's and Sammy's hearts, even their bodies and minds, into new, clean vessels through which He could pour Himself out onto others. Paul accepted Jesus' assignment to convert the Roman world and

Sammy accepted His call to minister to inner-city, under-privileged young people in southern California, that they, too, might be changed.

I can imagine Paul and Sammy singing:

> *All that I am*
> *All that I do*
> *I've given in to*
> *Life-giving truth*
> *I've come to believe*
> *I can be new*

SIX

tomorrow

Complacency can kill as a liar and a thief
Whispering thoughts of nagging tomorrows
Just beyond my reach
Its ever always subtleties seem harmless for
    the moment
Its venom is most bitter every time I give in

Complacency is danger in its purest form
It talks me into things to which I wouldn't otherwise
    conform
Given my ability to give in to the easy way
No wonder why my spirit hates my flesh

Tomorrow is much easier to deal with than today
But when tomorrow comes I still don't want to change
Why am I willing to replace a wealth of wonder
With a life of sure uncertainty
Tomorrow may not ever even be

How can I combat a complacent state of mind
I need a constant reminder of the wrong of wasted time
I need to train my heart in ways of seeing heaven
        as my home
I need to take the power given as my own

I know what's required of me
I want to do right
I want to do right

What is it that's keeping me from change

—Crystal Lewis

I've always been somewhat petite, never weighing more than a hundred pounds. And then I got pregnant. I gained fifty pounds with each of my two pregnancies. About nine months after Isabella was born, my body still retained more evidence of childbirth than I would have liked. So I decided to get serious about getting back in shape.

I bought nutrition books, weight training books, exercise books. I wanted to know the right way to go about this project. I started walking. The trick, for me, was finding the right time. My children were three years old and nine months old, so working out required extra effort.

I began this regimen in January, the middle of winter. Granted we live in California so I can't complain, but it was still a little cold for the kids to zoom along in a big, double jogger stroller as the morning breeze chilled their cheeks and froze their fingers.

So I decided to set my alarm and rise at six each morning to get a head start on my already early risers. I thought to myself, *Hey, if that woman in Proverbs 31 can get up before the crack of dawn, it can't be that hard.*

I was wrong. It was a challenge, to say the least, but my desire to reach my goal weight grew each day; therefore it became easier and easier each morning.

About six weeks or so into my new routine, the Holy Spirit convicted me of my lack of balance. I was concentrating on my physical appearance, but I was neglecting my spiritual life.

A Holy Awakening

For the past six weeks I had been more willing to endure the torture of getting up almost before the cows in Corona (a local agricultural community) to improve myself physically than I had been to get up early to improve myself spiritually. How could I do that? Why was I so driven to work on my weight and allow my spirit, my soul, to get lazy and flabby? How could I strive to maintain physical endurance when the spiritual endurance would ultimately sustain me?

I attend a women's Bible study at church on Friday mornings. A core group comes every time, but some women attend only periodically. It's a big church, so one Friday I sat next to someone I didn't know. Whether I knew her or not, I was determined she was going to hear about my frustration with myself. She barely sat down when I blurted how miserable I felt about my own spiritual laziness. "I mean, here I am getting up at six, willing to work like a dog to lose an extra fifteen pounds, and I'm not willing to get up to be with my Lord in the Word and prayer. What kind of Christian is that?"

"No biggie," she said, "just get up at five-thirty."

I gave her a very cold nod and a forced smile. Obviously she didn't know all my unique circumstances: two young kids (a full-time job), a husband to take care of (at least a full-time job), a career that requires traveling (the third full-time job), a ministry to maintain (and there's the fourth).

I stewed for most of that hour, then when the prayer requests came, she touched my hand and requested prayer for me (though she didn't use my name). By the end of that prayer, I knew she was right. I couldn't possibly give *400* percent of my life to those full-time jobs without the renewing, the refreshing, the comforting, the learning, and the strengthening that takes place in the presence of the Lord. I needed that time with Him. My excuses, my complacency, had kept me from the incomparable riches that are found in time spent with the King, and I vowed they wouldn't anymore!

How long do your resolutions last?

Longer than that one lasted for me, I'll bet.

I went home, grabbed the alarm clock, and was about to reset the time to five-thirty when I said to myself: *Let's celebrate my new resolve to get up early by staying in bed until six just one more time. Then I'll be all rested and raring to go tomorrow.*

I liked that. I was giving myself some time to get used to the idea, and I was sure that God, who loved me, would say it was a good idea too.

Well, God has His own alarm clocks.

The next morning, my daughter, ten-month-old Isabella, woke up in tears at five o'clock. She had been sleeping through the night since she was ten weeks old, and typically didn't get up until seven. Concerned, I got out of bed, walked down the hall, and as I reached her door, she stopped crying. Approaching the bed, I found her absolutely asleep. I climbed back into bed.

Not three minutes later, she began crying again. Once again, I forced myself out of bed and started down the hall. Silence. In fact, I could actually hear her snoring.

That's when it hit me. God was telling me something. I shook my head (*no, no, no, that just couldn't be*) and climbed right back into bed only to hear my alarm clock ring. It was fifteen minutes after five.

It must be broken, I thought. I turned the alarm off. It rang again. I'm not kidding. I started to laugh, then cry, then laugh again. God had my number, and that number was somewhere before five-thirty!

Verses Behind the Song

God has not given us a spirit of fear, but of power and of love and of a sound mind. (2 Tim. 1:7 NKJV)

Every Sunday I sat on the front row of my father's church (the back row as I got a little older) and watched as choir members filed into the sanctuary, their faces radiant, ready to fill the room with praises in the presence of the Lord.

When the choral "call to worship" fell to a triumphant silence, my father would invariably stand and grandly recite 2 Timothy 1:7, "For God has not given us a spirit of fear, but of *power* and of *love* and of a sound mind" (NKJV, emphasis added). I call this his life verse. It was not only a call to his congregation to live powerful, fearless lives for Christ, it was a call for himself to do the same.

In fact, the proof that this verse was working in his life was the fact that he was up there every Sunday. My dad is a thoughtful, usually soft-spoken man, a loving and gentle man with his share of patience (he let me live through my teens). Although he's a wonderful pastor, he's not one you'd expect in the spotlight. But that verse, that call to action, has taken and sustained him there.

This same verse has become a source of strength for me as well, and has significantly shaped my ministry. As I mentioned, my mom directed the church music and often used my voice within the service. My father suggested that before I sang I might want to say a few words about what the song meant to me—how I might apply its message to my life.

I replied, "You're kidding, right? I'm never going to be one of those singers who preaches to an audience. I sing. That's all."

Now it's hard to get me to stop talking. The Lord gave me a witness and a talent, and I'm determined to use both for His glory. That verse testifies to the power of His Spirit, which is responsible for what I do on—and off—stage.

Since it is such a powerful verse—and very much living and active as a two-edged sword—let's take it apart and look at each element more closely.

A Spirit of Fear

"God has not given us a spirit of fear . . ." The New King James Version uses the word *fear* in this verse. The New International Version uses the word *timidity*. Both words indicate apprehension about following through with a task. The Greek definition of the word *spirit* in the context of this verse is "mental disposition toward," so it can be said that,

"God didn't create us with a mental disposition toward fear or timidity . . ." We use fear as an excuse for complacency or to put off something we know God is asking us to do. We even disguise fear as something else because we're afraid someone will find out that we're afraid!

Yet Psalm 27:1 says, "The LORD is my light and my salvation— / whom shall I fear? / The LORD is the stronghold of my life— / of whom shall I be afraid?" And the beloved Twenty-third Psalm maintains: "Even though I walk / through the valley of the shadow of death, / I will fear no evil, / for you are with me" (v.4). These verses make it pretty clear that God doesn't want us to be afraid.

In fact, He created us with the capacity to be fearless! He so desires our fearlessness that He gives us a spirit of power to overcome our fears and our complacency! That power comes from God Himself.

A Spirit of Power

What kind of power are we talking about? Big power! Jesus told His followers when He sent seventy-two of them to do His work: "Behold, I give unto you power to tread on serpents and scorpions, and over all the power of the enemy: and nothing shall by any means hurt you" (Luke 10:19 KJV).

The word *power* in both 2 Timothy 1:7 and in this verse from Luke is the same. It means "force, ability, abundance, might, and strength."

God has given us the ability, and the strength to carry out His will for our lives. Whatever He asks us to do, in His name, by His power, we can do it. That's a fact.

God did not give us a spirit of fear, but of power and of a sound mind—all to overcome our fear of complacency.

And of a Sound Mind

Sometimes even simple circumstances throw us into a quandary, so we procrastinate. In the Greek, *sound mind* is defined by the words *discipline* and *self-control,* so we are also created with the capacity to be self-controlled.

When we are faced with a difficult decision, whether it be dealing with spiritual complacency, temptation, problems in our marriage, job, or school, we must remember that God allows us the privilege of going before Him with our complaints, concerns, and possibilities. Just as Martha's sister, Mary, found comfort and solace at Jesus' feet, we, too, find refreshment and restoration there as He provides the courage and power to think and act.

All too often my complacency keeps me from what is rightfully mine as a child of God: peace, joy, comfort, security, the abundant life. It always seems easier just to put things off until tomorrow. And as we put off those God-given tasks, the gap between us and our Master grows, forming a deep chasm with the turbulent action of guilt and fear. The longer we procrastinate, the greater the erosion—

and the longer we must wait to see the Lord in action with us. God wants to bridge the gap, erasing it altogether.

The morning that my ten-month-old daughter and the alarm clock woke me so *coincidentally* at about five, I got up. I went downstairs. I got my Bible and began to read and pray and cry. I laughed at the lengths to which God would go to get my attention. I cried at the lengths to which He had to go to get my attention. I felt almost like a prodigal. I had returned to a loving, forgiving Father. He openly embraced me in the knowledge and treasure of His Word.

Can you guess what verse I read first? It hit me like a ton of bricks. Second Timothy 1:7: "For God has not given us a spirit of fear, but of power and of love and of a sound mind" (NKJV). It was like hearing it for the first time. I so vividly realized that my excuses were simply the denial of my God-given ability to act fearlessly, with power and love, in self-discipline. There was absolutely no reason not to pursue both physical and spiritual growth, as long as I was aware that the spiritual nutrition was the most important.

Please know that my life does not consist of getting up at five o'clock every single morning. There are definitely days in which circumstances simply don't allow me the opportunity to do so. However, God wants our willingness. He wants us to put Him first. Sometimes that may mean having to give up that golf game or television program or shopping hour in the middle of the day to spend time alone with Him.

This experience changed my life. I hated running. Now I run a couple of miles several days a week. I love junk food. Now I know that I can't eat very much of it, depending on how badly I want to maintain all the work I've put into getting healthy. I realized that you can accomplish goals, like eating healthier, losing weight, and consistently exercising—but not without serious self-discipline.

Yet I've learned that time alone with God is the most valuable time available. Most important, I've learned that even Christians can fall into a life of excuses and complacency. The Word of God calls us to action. Don't be content to sit on the sidelines and watch. It's the equivalent of disobedience. Don't wait until tomorrow. Get up and into the game today.

SEVEN

return to me

I remember when
You first loved Me and
With Me was all you wanted to be

Now you've fallen in
To the lie within
Seems you're too far gone to come back to Me

Don't be discouraged dear one for My
Forgiveness awaits you here

Return to Me
Return to Me
I'm longing for the day when you will
Return to Me
Return to Me
I love you still

You defy Me
Yet you hide from Me

Our sacred vow was broken with another choice
As you're running
I'm still loving
Seems that you don't recognize My voice

I will continue crying calling
Until you hear Me say
Return to Me come back
My voice that was so familiar to you
Don't let it fade away

—Brian Ray and Crystal Lewis

All through high school Tierza was my best friend. And I mean *all* through. We met in our first freshman class, hit it off right away, and soon after, she came to our church youth group. After attending a few times, she thrilled me by responding to an altar call, taking Jesus as her Savior.

Over the next four years we were inseparable. Of course, we talked more about boys and parties than spiritual issues, but I had no doubt—we were both Christians. Who would want to be at church that much if they weren't? After graduation, Tierza went away to college and then on to a dream job in Florida working for a resort while I got busy with my career and finally my family. We would talk only a couple of times a year. Certainly not enough to keep a friendship going, but enough to let each other know we still cared.

Not long ago I telephoned her to see how she was doing.

"Oh, fine," she said, "but there's this Jesus freak who's moved in next door, and he's driving me nuts. You'd think the way this guy talks he'd been nailed to the cross right beside Him. (Sigh) I wish he had been! He won't leave me alone.

"There's nothing but old ladies and Bible-thumpers down here. You'd think with all the humidity they'd rot, but they don't. They just keep driving bad and talking."

Our conversation ended soon after that, and when I dropped the phone onto the cradle my heart had turned to lead. *Jesus freaks? Bible-thumpers?* How far had she fallen away? Christ used to be the center of our lives. Now, for Tierza, Christ was just an interruption, at best someone to ridicule. I felt an ache grow in my heart. If it hurt me to hear her talk like that, I wondered how Jesus must feel.

The image of Him standing on a hill the last time He entered Jerusalem, weeping over the lost souls there— those He had been unable to reach during His ministry— burned in my mind. I could almost hear the anguish in His voice as He cried, "O Jerusalem . . . how often I have longed to gather your children together, as a hen gathers her chicks under her wings, but you were not willing!" (Luke 13:34).

After hanging up the phone, I sat at the kitchen table for quite a while, worrying about her and praying for her. And wondering what had happened to change Tierza like that. Maybe we weren't saved during those high school years. Maybe we were just kidding ourselves.

Searching my memory, I looked for proof one way or the other. I thought back to the unchristian things we had done as teens. Like copying each other's homework, or covering for each other while we lied to our parents.

I actually became excited when I remembered a time that our Christianity stopped us from cheating on a biology final. We went so far as to start hiding crib notes in our clothing. Then we stopped, looked at each other, and decided it just wasn't right. We ended up passing. Not with the grades we had hoped for but that was OK. Sure I was saved. At the four Christian summer camps I went to during my high school years, I went up during each altar call, just to make sure—and Tierza went with me. Sure she was a Christian.

Still maybe she wasn't saved. Maybe for whatever reason she had only been my spiritual shadow those years. After all, we don't see the motives of the heart, so there's no way to be sure. And now that she had fallen away, maybe she would never return to Christ.

I know it's impossible to lose our salvation. Romans 8 makes that perfectly clear. But it is possible for kids and adults alike to be part of a Christian fellowship and not be saved. John explains this to the early church: "They went out from us, but they did not really belong to us. For if they had belonged to us, they would have remained with us; but their going showed that none of them belonged to us" (1 John 2:19).

Kids might come to the Christian youth group just because they want a place to belong. And some parents come to church only because of their kids. They want their kids safe from dangerous temptations, and in a real sense they want to choose their friends for them. Youth groups offer parents and kids a *temptation-free zone*. But the parents are also hoping that over time their kids will develop a spiritual insulation from the corruption of the world. The parents know they could have used that kind of insulation, and with any luck at all, the kids will obtain it through a kind of osmosis. The good news about these goals is that sometimes both parents and kids respond to the gospel message and get saved. Sometimes, they don't.

Adults also become part of a fellowship for reasons of their own. A husband might go because his wife does. Or a wife because of her husband. Or maybe they want to be seen in church for career or political reasons. Or their friends are going and they, like the teens, want to belong. Or they've gone to church all their lives; why stop now?

Sometimes the reasons are emotional—they feel less

guilty about the rest of the week if they sit in a church pew for an hour on Sunday. Or their lives are unbearably chaotic, except for the few hours at church on Sunday morning. Or they just feel guilty or frightened if they don't go.

There are no bad reasons for going to church. God gets His people there any number of ways. And, if they are His people, over time they hear the gospel and respond to salvation's call. But there are other people who respond to everything else, to all the church trappings—the committees, the ministries, even the evangelistic efforts—without responding to the gospel.

My fear for Tierza was that she was one of those. I became even more frightened for her when I thought she might be like one of those spoken of in Hebrews 6:4–6:

> *It is impossible for those who have once been enlightened, who have tasted the heavenly gift, who have shared in the Holy Spirit, who have tasted the goodness of the word of God and the powers of the coming age, if they fall away, to be brought back to repentance, because to their loss they are crucifying the Son of God all over again and subjecting him to public disgrace.*

Yet even as I worried about Tierza I found hope. I remembered a friend (I'll call him Barry) who is in his fifties now. When Barry was eight his grandmother, who was a Christian, paid for him to go to Christian camp. His parents allowed him to go even though they weren't Christians. He believes he was saved there. Barry remembers his cousins being there and arguing with him about his salvation. They wanted nothing to do with it. In fact, one of them even slapped him when he talked about Jesus working in his heart.

The fight with his cousins actually got so heated, Barry called his parents and asked them to pick him up that night. Not wanting his worldly psyche to suffer any more Christian indignities, the parents were there like a shot. To ease his transition back from "the land of the cults," his parents even treated him to his favorite thing, a drive-in movie. The memory of that whole camp salvation experience is still so vivid, to this day Barry remembers the movie: *The Pony Express* with Charlton Heston.

But since Barry was only eight and his parents were not Christians (although his mother is now), he grew up not thinking much about Jesus. In fact, when he looks back on his life, he doesn't see much Christian living at all. Oh, he went to church, but it was a dead denomination preaching a social gospel. If asked he would say that he believed there was a God, but he would have been hard-pressed to define Him. Barry's only emotional tie with the Lord came during his favorite movie, *Ben-Hur* (which he saw often). During the scene where Jesus was nailed to the cross, the cross was raised, then dropped into the hole, he always cried.

After a divorce, Barry all but abandoned his two children in northern California by coming to the southland. But once here, he quickly met a Christian lady and fell in love. She insisted he go to church and he consented. After all, he had been going to churches all his life. Well, this church preached the true gospel. Within a few weeks, Barry returned to the Lord and recommitted his life to Jesus. He now has a thriving ministry. He and his wife are also *wonderfully* married, as he puts it. He now has a good relationship with the two children from his first marriage—and even has five grandchildren.

My hope is that Tierza will also return to the Lord.

When speaking of hell, D. L. Moody, the great turn-of-the-century evangelist, would often be in tears. He cried for the lost, for the souls of those who would not respond to his message. He cried for those who would leave his service and never think about the Lord again. Not me. So often I find myself just glad I'm saved and that the Lord did a miracle in my heart. So often I'm not thinking about the lost at all.

Shame on me.

But now, as I think about Tierza and so many others who professed Christ's death and resurrection so fervently as kids and are now walking away from Him, I, too, want to cry. As I imagine Jesus cries. That's why, when I spoke to Tierza this last time, I sat down and wrote "Return to Me."

Verses Behind the Song

A farmer went out to sow his seed. As he was scattering the seed, some fell along the path; it was trampled on, and the birds of the air ate it up. Some fell on rock, and when it came up, the plants withered because they had no moisture. Other seed fell among thorns, which grew up with it and choked the plants. Still other seed fell on good soil. It came up and yielded a crop, a hundred times more than was sown. (Luke 8:5–8)

When we study the parable of the sower, we quickly learn that the seeds being sown were the Word of God. And they were sprinkled over four types of people. One type, symbolized by the path, never received the seed at all. They were hardened against it, mocking it, fighting it, or completely ignoring it. Today, some might excuse this behavior by calling the offer of salvation a crutch or scientifically unworthy of their attentions or just foolishness. Or protest that it's just trying to enslave them and turn them into glassy-eyed do-gooders. Sometimes they're quite polite about it. "No, thank you, I really don't care about such things." But in the final analysis, the soil is not prepared, and the seed just lies on the surface as bird food.

The next two types of people seem to listen to the Word—at first. In one case the seed fell on rock, where the root quickly sprouted and the plant shot up, but in the heat of the day, withered. The plant, of course, refers to our belief, which is withering, and when that happens, the person leaves the fellowship. These folks come and go so fast we only remember them from the attendance cards they filled out. They show up on our list of those we "just must call and invite back" for the next several years. But they never return our calls. They're like ghosts from the past—in our prayers but little else.

The seed produced fruit that lasted a while. It fell on soil that hadn't been divinely prepared but had nutrients enough to keep the plant alive for a while. In this soil a form of belief grew and bloomed, but the cares of the world acted like thorns and choked the belief out.

This third type of person reminds me of another close friend from our youth group, Don, who was a member from sixth grade through junior high. He loved music. He knew all the words and all the moves and gestures, and he sang along with everything and everybody. During high school he played the piano and sang. Although he didn't have the knack for writing music, he could take an existing song and put a spin on it that would make it truly unique. We had so much in common, including our Christianity. Don certainly showed as much evidence of his salvation as I did of mine, and he did respond to an altar call at one of our Sunday morning services.

A couple of years ago, Don announced that he was a

homosexual and that he had serious problems with the Christian position on the issue.

I loved Don (and still do) as much as I love any friend. Now I'm deeply and genuinely afraid for him. God makes no bones about the fact that homosexuality is wrong. He created men and women, and He created the man to be with the woman and the woman to be with the man. The book of Leviticus makes homosexuality a capital offense, and Romans says that homosexual activity is terribly offensive to God.

But the Lord also wants us to love the homosexual as we love everybody else. If there is anyone on this earth who needs the Lord's love, it's the homosexual because of a deep-seated confusion and conflict.

I think one of the great failures of the church is its reaction to AIDS sufferers. Too often, and I include myself, we are just relieved it isn't happening to us when we should be showing these people the love of Christ through our involvement in their suffering.

So I fear for Don—I fear that his brush with Christianity was only a brush—I fear that his lifestyle will cost him his life. I pray for him often.

The final type of person in this parable was truly saved. The seed landed on divinely prepared soil and sank deep where it was nourished by the Spirit and grew to produce a whole bunch of fruit. One fruit is the ability to love unselfishly. We don't love that way as a matter of course, but we strive to. And that's the love we have for our friends. I love Tierza and Don, and I want the best for them. And that best is a life filled with good and godly things. Why? Because such a life is evidence of God's blessing. And such a life will garner even more of God's blessings as it unfolds. And such a life ends with being present with the Lord forever.

We, of course, hope that every one of our friends belongs to this last category. We hope that they are true believers and headed with us to heaven. But to suspect that a friend is not heaven-bound also produces the purest of heartaches. Instead of being secure in the arms of Jesus, they're headed down a road that literally leads to destruction, and that is not only upsetting, but frightening. Another parable tells that story: the parable of the prodigal son.

The Prodigal

Imagine you were one of the people who saw the prodigal son when he was tending the pigs. What would you have thought of him? Not much, I suspect. He was just a hired hand, and probably not a very good one, given his past history of wanting something for nothing. You probably wouldn't see anything of his father in him, either. No trappings of wealth—the rich clothing, the jewelry, the confident bearing. No sense of authority. He probably hadn't bathed in a while, and at this stage in his journey, defeat flourished in his eyes.

That's the way it is with those who've fallen away. Right now, I find it hard to distinguish Tierza or Don from most everyone else in the world. Just as it was hard to distinguish them from all the other kids who professed their separation from the world when they were in the youth group. So what does this mean?

It means that had I not known Tierza and Don before, my prayer for them would be the same as for any unsaved person. I would pray that God would prepare their hearts' soil. I'd pray that the seeds of the gospel might be planted and nourished by the Spirit and that those seeds might germinate, and as a result, they might come to know Jesus as their Lord and Savior.

But I do know Tierza and Don. I do know they've heard the gospel and have at one time responded to the message, and I do know that they are now walking away from the Lord. My prayer for them is a little different. It's that they might return, that they might seek again the blessing of salvation.

Do you have friends who have fallen away? I can't imagine that you don't. What is your reaction to them? I know my first reaction was to write them off. As I spoke to Tierza, I felt betrayed. I was a Jesus freak to her, a Bible-thumper, a gullible idiot. She insulted me. What is your reaction to being insulted? Mine is to strike back with something like: "Well, you're the gullible idiot. Jesus freak doesn't begin to describe the kind of freak you are." But in this case, rather than striking out, the perfect revenge is just to say nothing: keep the gospel to myself and literally let her boil in her own juices.

But there's another reaction. It's saying to yourself: "Oh, well, it's their problem. They had their chance and they blew it." For me, that voice came from my feeling of rejection. Both Tierza and Don have rejected my most cherished belief. And in doing so, they have rejected who I am and everything I stand for.

But you and I both know we can't say either of these things. We have to swallow our pride, perhaps a little anger and indifference, and begin to pray. We also need to maintain those relationships if at all possible, taking the opportunities God presents to present God—in the form of Jesus and His work on the cross.

Or maybe *you* are the one who has fallen away.

Only you know your heart. Take a look at it now. Do you know Jesus Christ as your Lord and Savior? Are you proactive in your Christianity? Sure we can always do more, or that's the theory anyway. But you know if you're walking and working with Jesus. If you are, then praise the Lord.

But maybe there's a part of your life that's fallen away. Maybe you're harboring sin or nurturing a point of pride. Something is holding a part of you back from full communion with the Lord. Confess it to Him today, and repent of it. If it takes counseling, do the radical spiritual surgery necessary to get rid of the obstacle and return that part of your life to full fellowship with Him.

Or maybe you have fallen away completely and have picked up this album and book because—well, for whatever reason. Maybe you used to be close to the Lord, but now you don't think about Him much. Or when you do, your rebellion is keeping the upper hand. It doesn't matter which or why. It only matters that you begin praying for help to get you back to Him. And don't pray alone. Call a Christian friend and get him or her praying with you too. I know I'd be thrilled to get that kind of call from Tierza or Don. Or talk to a pastor about what you're feeling and going through. This Sunday, attend a church nearby—and when you feel comfortable begin the appropriate dialogue with those who can help.

And while you're doing all that, listen to your heart—listen for Jesus whispering in your spiritual ear. He's saying:

> *Return to Me*
> *I'm longing for the day when you will*
> *Return to Me*
> *Return to Me*
> *I love you still*

EIGHT

be with him

But Jesus comes to me
While I watch and wait
And long for peace

He is always there
It's where I belong
For the road I'm on is long

Be with Him
I'll be with Him
Until the day I die

And Jesus comes to me
He's my everything
He's all I need

And His voice I hear
He's opened up my eyes
It's clear the reason why

And Jesus comes to me
He's my everything
He's all I need

And on the day I die
Jesus comes to lead me on
Taking me home with Him
Where I'll be with Him
Be with Him
Be with Him
Forever

I'll always
Be with Him
Be with Him
Always forever

—Brian Ray

a dear friend wrote me a letter in the form of a story. For her, writing it was therapeutic. Sharing it with me and getting my sympathetic reaction helped her deal with her loss. Since her story was instrumental to Brian writing "Be With Him," I wanted to share her letter with you:

My name is Meg and I'm the Chief Executive Officer of my family: one husband, three kids, who are eight and younger, two dogs, a fish, and an aging father—well, the memory of an aging father, who, up until a few days ago, required constant care.

I call myself the CEO because the execution of the plan my husband and I came up with a while ago falls mostly to me. After all, I am the oldest of five children (three girls and two boys), so my husband and I felt it was our responsibility to look after my dad when he developed a semiserious case of loneliness after my mom died a few years ago.

I missed her, too, which was probably why Dad felt so comfortable calling to talk about her and their life together. As the months built one on another, he called more often—finally four times a day, sometimes more. I didn't mind the frequency of the calls all that much. It was the desperation I began to hear in his voice that concerned me. And hanging up was becoming more and more difficult for him. It was as if speaking to me kept her alive and hanging up was like pulling the plug. And he loved her far too much to ever do that.

His health was failing too. He'd been using a wheelchair since a few months after her death and his breathing was getting more labored. He seemed to pull air into himself like one might pull water from a very deep well. Truth be told, we felt somewhat obligated at first, me being the firstborn, and us being the only family. One sister and one brother were married, no children or permanent dwellings as of yet, and the other brother and sister were both single and, well, still restless. We have a nice home and an extra room if our boys share one. Plus our income could easily support an extra person. So Dad moved in six months after Mom died.

My children have always been fond of their papa, even though my folks lived a distance away and only visited a couple of times a year. I guess grandparents don't have to visit a lot to be grandparents. They just get to be. While parents have to be parents all the time.

Anyway, the kids wouldn't leave him alone when he first moved in. They climbed on his bed, begged for rides on his lap in the wheelchair, all but dressed him up in doll clothes. They loved to help me fix his food and serve it to him, sometimes in bed, sometimes at the table. Every Sunday they fought over who would sit next to him during church.

Aah, church! The very same church that I'd grown up in. The same church that Dad pastored when I was a little girl. Not many remembered him personally, but when he started coming it was an occasion. He'd pastored there for many years and everyone thought it wonderful that he had come back during these fading years.

Occasionally, probably to relive my youth, I would sit in the same seat that I did as a kid. And afterward, on the way home, I'd hear Dad telling my kids exactly what he'd told me: "Stand up for Jesus, as He stood up for you. Live for Him, be with Him daily, that you might be with Him forever." Oh, I loved listening to him. There was such strength in those words. Is it the same when you listen to your dad, Crystal? It probably is. It's like God is sitting right there with you and He's sharing eternal, time-tested wisdom with you. Not because He has an obligation to, but because He loves you more than you will ever know.

Well, as time passed, my kids got used to Papa being around. They played with him a little less, took fewer wheelchair rides, didn't help fix his meals at all, and often forgot to say goodnight to him, although he never forgot to say goodnight to them. Most of the time Dad would just sit silently in "his chair" and read and nap and read and eat and read and nap again. What he read mostly was the Bible.

And of course, it brought back the childhood memory of him sitting in his chair every morning praying and reading the Word. I feel so sorry for kids nowadays who grow up without fathers. They're so important. So much of an anchor to the family. And to see them show obedience to God—well—it's such an important witness. To see a man bow his head and thank God for that which God has provided—including his children. To have someone thank God for me! How could I not sit for hours and listen to his advice? Even in these fading years. His body might be falling apart, but his mind was still sharp.

About a week ago, just before the "get to school rush," he spoke those familiar words to me: "Stand up for Jesus, as He stood up for you. Live for Him, be with Him daily that you might be with Him forever." I absently nodded something back to him just as the kids came clamoring down the stairs. Everyone scrambled for his or her lunch box and homework, tripping over the dogs, the wheelchair and toys left on the floor. We headed for the car, each child kissing Papa good-bye—throwing their lips at him as if there might be some luck involved in actually connecting.

I didn't bother to kiss him. I was a little old to be doing that sort of thing when I was just going to be gone a few minutes. "Good-bye, beautiful!" I heard him say as I began to pull the door shut. "I love you! I'll see you when you come home."

I was gone only a few minutes but in that few minutes my father died.

After the funeral, I came home to a house that was a little emptier. Believe me, my father never occupied much space. But his passing left a huge void. He brought a lot of joy when he came. But more than joy, he brought the rock-solid sense of God being right there in the room with us.

I sat in his chair after the funeral and stared across the room at the wheelchair. Now, a wheelchair is the symbol of weakness, of disability. But there was nothing weak or imperfect about his godly witness to us and the words he proclaimed. Those words rang with the promise of forever, heralding the King of kings, the Creator Himself!

My mom and dad dedicated their lives to God's service and told anyone who would listen that knowing God is the greatest of privileges—and knowing Him would allow you to be with Him forever. Now they are both living the truth of that proclamation.

Oh, how much do I owe them both? How much do I owe God

for allowing me to reap the benefit of their obedience? Can my debt ever be counted? How wealthy am I? Knowing them. Knowing God through them. Can those riches ever be counted?

Sitting there (in his chair) and now to you, I promise I will pass that legacy on to my children.

Not long after receiving this letter, Brian wrote "Be With Him."

Verses Behind the Song

For I am convinced that neither death nor life, neither angels nor demons, neither the present nor the future, nor any powers, neither height nor depth, nor anything else in all creation, will be able to separate us from the love of God that is in Christ Jesus our Lord. (Rom. 8:38–39)

Two verses give the essence of "Be With Him." We'll see the second one later, but this first one is the clearest statement of God's inseparability from us that exists in Scripture. Nothing can sever the ties we have with Christ. Nothing. Once He has saved us, once the gavel has come down in God's court of law and pronounced us *just,* nothing can undo what has been done. We are His as we have been from the foundation of the world and will be forever.

Meg's father knew that as well as anyone. As the dearest

parts of his life slowly left him alone in that chair, he knew that God—in the form of His Word and his loving daughter Meg—would be with him until his last breath.

Of course, this is true for us too. I can almost bet that right now you're facing a trial of some sort. It might be a small one. Just something that is irritating you, or causing you some worry. Maybe someone at work who has been a friend is now beginning to act standoffish. Or maybe something your child said has you a little worried. It could be any number of things, but it's gnawing at you and you don't know what to do about it.

Or perhaps it's not so small. Maybe like Meg, you're facing the death of a loved one. Or you got laid off. Maybe you came to listen to *Gold* and read this companion to it because you need the solace something like this might give.

Whatever you're going through right now, Jesus is right there with you.

You know that already. I'm not telling you anything new. But it could be in the past you took things to the Lord and were dissatisfied with what you got back. Maybe the situation got worse instead of better. Or it didn't turn out the way you wanted it to. Or you sensed you were being asked to do something you just couldn't bring yourself to do. And over time you decided it was best just to handle these things yourself. For we sinners who still have the remnants of the world flowing through us, it's an easy conclusion.

Finding Strength in Weakness

An essential part of knowing God is with us, is surrendering to His lead and His will. Elijah, during the three-year drought, was commanded to stay with a widow at Zarephath. When he got there he told the widow to prepare him bread to eat. But she told him she had but a handful of flour and only a little oil left. In fact, she was planning to fix the last of it for her son and then die of starvation. Elijah told her that if she prepared the bread for him, using the last of her food, her flour and her oil would never run out. In faith, she did as she was commanded and he kept his promise (see 1 Kings 18:9–24). Sometimes God tests our faith first, and then gives us all things.

Surrender is an essential part of the Christian faith. If there is any reluctance on your part, do as Meg's father did—surrender to Christ and He will see you through.

But, in the final analysis, didn't Meg's father have to endure death alone?

From the story you might conclude that. But not so. As I read Meg's letter, I felt that the end of her father's earthly existence had been orchestrated so that he might die in the sole company of the One who loved him most—Jesus.

A second truth also shines through Meg's father's life:

You are the light of the world. A city on a hill cannot be hidden.
Neither do people light a lamp and put it under a bowl. Instead

*they put it on its stand, and it gives light to everyone in the
house. In the same way, let your light shine before men, that
they may see your good deeds and praise your Father in
heaven. (Matt. 5:14–16)*

As Meg's dad's life fires began to dim, Christ's fire within
him shone that much brighter. The Lord tells us that His
strength is shown in our weakness. As our eyesight fails, as
our limbs falter, as our heart beats toward the end, God
appears ever so strong. But what makes this so? How can
God appear so strong in a trembling voice? Or shine so
brilliantly in cloudy eyes?

Because the "fruit of God's Spirit" never withers. Love, joy,
peace, patience, kindness, goodness, faithfulness, gentleness,
and self-control (see Gal. 5:22). These are the results of our
long-term relationship with Jesus and they are evident in
every part of our lives. Even sitting there in his chair, Meg's
father exhibited these divine traits.

He waited as peacefully and patiently for the care he
received from Meg as he did for Jesus to come and take him
home. There was no rancor, no raging against his infirmity
and his own mortality. In fact, he was regal in his peaceful-
ness, majestic in his patience, although everyone would
have understood if he had been irritable. Surely he had
been active all his life and then was reduced to sitting,
reading, and being waited on. Some might find such an end

degrading, even humiliating. But he was joyful, kind, and gentle, taking the love of those around him without complaint, even when the expression of their love began to fade. Goodness? Self-control? I have known people who came to the end of their road so angry they constantly snapped at those around them, creating hostility everywhere they went. From Meg's father came only goodness, for even in the inevitable times of melancholy he exercised self-control.

Finally, Meg's father showed love and faithfulness. In his final words to Meg, both blazed through him like the sun on a clear summer's day. "Stand up for Jesus, as He stood up for you. Live for Him, be with Him daily, that you might be with Him forever." Her father showed love by stressing one of God's greatest truths to her, thus giving her a most precious gift—the only one he had left to give. And he showed love for Jesus as he believed every word He said. He showed faithfulness to his daughter as a good father. Good fathers lead their children even when their legs are too weak to walk. And he showed faithfulness to the Lord he loved, because to the end, he proclaimed God in the only way he knew how to the only audience he was given.

Praise God for fathers like Meg's—and fathers like mine—and I pray, fathers like yours.

But this shining light is not unique to fathers. It's in all of us who have taken Jesus Christ as our personal Lord and

Savior. And our job as Christians is to take a nice clean rag and shine that light every day so it becomes a bright beacon.

Why?

First Peter 3:15 puts it this way: "But in your hearts set apart Christ as Lord. Always be prepared to give an answer to everyone who asks you to give the reason for the hope that you have."

Our lights are to shine so brightly through the normal living of our lives that those around us will be inclined to ask us our spiritual secret.

The other day I was grocery shopping with the kids. Isabella sat in the cart's child seat while Solomon hung on the side. It was late in the afternoon and the open checkout stands were all jammed with full carts. Two overflowing ones were right in front of us. The kids had already spotted all the candy they'd be near soon and were anxiously, and loudly, choosing what they wanted, their selections changing rapidly. Suddenly something inexplicable happened. The checkout stand next to me had only one shopper with a small load. I quickly pushed my full cart around and nosed toward it. I was just about to make the turn into that line when another cart, pushed by a woman with two kids, barreled around me and took the place I'd been aiming at. "Excuse me!" she barked.

"Sorry, I was just going over to this other checkout stand."

"But I said I was going to that checkout stand!"

"But I didn't hear you."

"I said it three times!" Another bark.

"But I didn't hear you."

"I said it to my children." A nasty bark—and she was firmly planted in the checkout line. I swallowed the urge to say anything back and returned to the line I'd been in.

"I'd have killed her," came a whisper from behind.

"Well," I said, to the woman standing there, "she's probably had a rough day." Solomon was waving a Snickers bar in front of me. "I guess the Lord's not giving her the strength He's giving me." I took the Snickers from Solomon's hand. "You know you're supposed to ask politely for things."

I am convinced that trials often come not so much to test us, but so that others might view Christ through the window opened by our godly response.

Maybe your response to the trials you're going through right now will be an encouragement to someone close to you. Or to someone you don't even know. Take a moment and sense Jesus' presence in your life. Sense Him right there in the room with you. Sense Him working everything out in your life for your good. Now wrap your spiritual arms around Him and sense His arms around you. And then surrender the trial—and your will—to Him and let Him lead you along the way.

Let Him be with you as you commit to "Be With Him."

NINE

what about god?

What about God
What about God
Where am I
That I don't feel Him anymore

Can a man go so far
That he doesn't feel the presence of his closest
     friend

What about God
What about God
Where am I
That I don't see Him working anymore

Can a man go so far
That he doesn't feel the presence of his closest friend

Can a man go so far
He doesn't feel the presence of his only friend

What about God
What about God
What about God
What about God
What about God
What about Him

—Brian Ray

*M*etro One, our recording company, has only a few employees, but they're the greatest. They're smart, they work hard, and we would be hard-pressed to do all the things we do without them. Our office is on the second floor of a two-story building, which frankly needed some work when we bought it. Wanting the best for our employees and more inspirational surroundings for ourselves, we decided to redecorate. Actually, it was more like *rebuild*.

Of course, we decided to do this in the middle of producing *Gold*.

Suddenly we were dealing with interior designers and buyers and choosing colors and assigning potential offices. To properly set up computers we had to make sure the wiring was adequate and outlets were in the proper places. The list went on forever and the beat goes on to this day. The album is ready, but our offices are not.

Martin Luther probably wrote some of the greatest

hymns of all time in a stone room with a quill pen—or was he still scratching on clay? Our environment really doesn't matter. Having a nice place to work is wonderful since we're there so much of the time, but after a while, much of what's going on becomes a distraction.

I mentioned computers. I know nothing about computers, but they're supposed to be easy to learn and use; windows pop up all over the screen, telling us what to do and what not to do. Well, I have written a lot of stuff, and I can't figure out how to get it printed. It just won't print, and I've been working on that for nearly an hour.

Distractions. All of them keeping us from the presence of God, our closest Friend.

Distractions Play on Distractions

The other evening our family sat down to dinner. With a four-year-old and a two-year-old, that can be an interesting experience! But after a while we were all situated, and Brian and I bowed our heads to say the blessing.

Well, I didn't bow my head all the way. I tilted my head to the side, watching Solomon and Isabella with an open right eye to make sure they were praying with us. Usually they're pretty good about it. Their heads go down and their little hands go up, clasped in front of their noses, and they listen.

But that night Solomon seemed to be more interested in prying the bottom of his plate off the table with his fork.

Brian got just past the "Dear Lord, bless . . ." when I barked, "We're trying to pray," at Solomon.

Brian jumped, Solomon jumped, the plate all but spun in the air and the fork clattered on the floor. I just had to laugh. Here we were going before our Savior as a family— I was barking, and forks were flying. Solomon's distraction had distracted me from what was truly important—showing my son the gentleness of God when He brings us back into focus. I should have simply laid my hand on Solomon's hand and steered his attention back to his father's prayer.

But sometimes the distractions are more far-reaching, and getting refocused isn't so easy.

I always find it peculiar when I hear of or see someone who has fallen away from the Lord. What enticed them away? What offer seemed more attractive? What distractions caught their focus and kept it? I'm typically surprised by the answers, for the distractions are usually quite obvious. (Satan tends to use the same old tricks to keep us from the truth. On one hand this might seem stupid, and yet the fact that we keep falling for the same tricks speaks volumes about our stupidity not his.) The distractions are often things we've fallen prey to many times before. Things we can't seem to defeat: one more drink, one more date. We get suckered into thinking, *One more,* which turns into, *This isn't so bad.* Soon the guilt is buried.

One thing I've learned about distractions is that the distraction itself becomes the thing or person we blame for our falling away. It's as though we say, "Ahh! What a relief to have something or someone to blame." The only problem is that it's a lie! We are responsible for our actions, words, and choices. When we become complacent or distracted in our relationships with the Lord it is because we chose to. The saddest part is that the farther we fall away, the more unrecognizable His voice becomes.

One of the intriguing things about God is that He made us people of choice. He created us with the ability to choose Him, but He also allowed the world to compete for our focus. The burden rests on our shoulders to deny the world access to our hearts and focus on the things of God (see Col. 3:2).

It was while considering the power of distractions and the unfortunate fact that so many give in to that power that the lyrics to "What About God" surfaced.

Verses Behind the Song

But the worries of this life, the deceitfulness of wealth and the desires for other things come in and choke the word, making it unfruitful. (Mark 4:19)

Samson was blessed by God. From the moment he was conceived he was set apart by the Lord to do special things. As the angel of the Lord put it to his parents: "He will begin the deliverance of Israel from the hands of the Philistines" (Judg. 13:5). And he was given the wherewithal to do just that. He was brave, unbelievably strong, and brash. And although he was the very person to pull that off, no one in Scripture was more distracted.

First he was distracted by a beautiful Philistine woman, Timnah, when he should have found a wife from his own people. This distraction led to Timnah's betrayal of Samson to her Philistine friends, and Samson killed thirty people because of it. He then lost Timnah to another man. Instead of learning from this experience and returning to his duties as judge to the Israelites, Samson was again distracted. After discovering he had lost Timnah, he angrily torched the Philistines' standing grain. This led to Samson's slaughter of even more Philistines.

Not long after that entered Delilah, and we all know the story of her betrayal. In the end, tied to the Philistines' temple pillars, Samson's life was reduced to a simple though remarkable act of revenge—taking as many Philistines with him to eternity as he could.

Although God was with him along the way, no one could ever accuse Samson of leading a triumphant life.

Finding Your Life Goal

But how do we live such lives? And how do we keep from being distracted so we can live such a life?

One reason Samson didn't lead a victorious life was that leading it wasn't his goal. In fact, as we read this passage, it's hard to determine Samson's goal. His life was a hodgepodge of events strung together without any clear sense of direction or purpose. He seemed to accomplish what God had in mind—the beginning of Israel's separation from the Philistines—in spite of himself, rather than because of his actions. This realization leads us to conclude: to eliminate distractions in our Christian walk, the first thing we need is a *life goal*.

Of course, the Lord came up with one for us: "'Love the Lord your God with all your heart and with all your soul and with all your mind.' This is the first and greatest commandment. And the second is like it: 'Love your neighbor as yourself'" (Matt. 22:37–39).

But God made me a unique individual. Although these commandments serve as a firm foundation, I wanted to build my own overall goal on top of it. So I said, "I will place God first in all things, then my family and my ministry."

Lofty words, eh? And there's something about them that elicits the response, "Sure, but that goes without saying." But it *doesn't* go without saying. As soon as I said it, I could no longer ignore it. Saying it gave it validity. This life goal became the measuring stick for everything I do.

Just as an experiment, and just for a few minutes, make my goal your goal. Say it to yourself, maybe write it down.

Now make a list of things you have done today. Be as detailed as you like. Then check off the things that don't fit. Can you find anything?

I know I can find some things that don't fit in my own day. One of them happened about six this morning. A week ago we spent several days recording one of the songs for the *Gold* album. Last night I had the chance to listen to the final cut—the fully mixed, ready-to-go version that would eventually find its way onto the album. After listening to it a couple of times, I decided something about it just didn't seem right. I couldn't put my finger on the problem then.

But after sleeping on it all night, something occurred to me. Instead of reading my Bible, praying, and meditating as I try to do every morning, I had skipped it all and headed right to the recording. Well, that wasn't the right thing to do. Had I taken my morning schedule and measured it against my overall goal, I would have spent the necessary time with the Lord, then tackled the recording as it fit into the priority scheme for the rest of my day. After all, the Lord is in control. I didn't have to be anxious about the recording. If something needed attention, I would find it. And finding it a couple of hours later wouldn't matter at all.

None of us are perfect and it's hard to take every little interruption and measure our reaction to it against our overall, life-defining goal. So there will be times when we find ourselves ranging far afield, not sure how we got there.

Not long ago I was approached by someone at church to help in a fund-raising campaign for a new building. It was going to be a big effort with a lot of people involved, and because I'm something of a celebrity they thought I would be of value to the effort. I agreed to participate. Well, it was more than just participation, it was a full-time commitment! They handed me a list of people to see personally that was as long as my arm. They gave me a list of meetings to attend that was equally as long. And then there were forms to fill out, instructions on what to do with this donation or that one, and the names of people with whom to coordinate. Before I knew it my life had changed. I was no longer a singer who spoke occasionally to her audience. I was a banker for the Lord. And the bigger the banker I became, the less of a mother and wife and singer I was.

But there was more.

When I worked hard to fulfill my overall goals in light of my priorities (don't I sound like someone getting ready for a corporate planning session?), I was on fire for Christ. But since I was doing something I was ill-prepared and equipped to do, I woke up each morning feeling already defeated. I became grumpy, guilty, and at odds with just about everyone.

I was at odds with the fund-raisers because they were keeping me from those things I loved most. I was at odds with my family and those at the ministry, because I felt guilty for shortchanging them. And I was at odds with the Lord, because He was letting all this happen and causing me a bunch of stress I didn't need.

After I thought and prayed about it for a while, I realized the Lord hadn't caused a thing. It was me. I had allowed myself to be distracted from those things most important to me. Of course, had I had the time, the energy, and the inclination to be a fund-raiser, all would have been fine. Fund-raising is a church activity, and church is certainly on the priority list. But it's not ahead of my relationship with the Lord or my children or my husband or my music ministry. I decided to get things back in focus, so I resigned from that activity.

So, if you're feeling discouraged, or at odds with coworkers, you can be sure that God has given you different stewardship items, different talents, and different gifts from the ones you're using. He's given you different burdens. My sister has a burning desire to work in the inner city and she's ordering her life to make a contribution to the Lord there.

The questions you need to ask yourself are: What are my burdens, what talents do I have, who are the people, and what are the things over which the Lord has given me responsibility? And with those answers in mind, what are my goals? So that when you order your day, and, on a grander scale your life, you can be faithful to the goal.

When you start living this way, you'll be amazed at how much energy and purpose you will possess. And the reason is simple—never again will you be asking the question: *What about God?*

TEN

lord, i believe in you

Though I can't see
Your holy face
And Your throne in heaven above
It seems so far away

Though I can't touch
Your nail-scarred hands
I have a deep and unspeakable joy
That makes my faith to stand

Lord I believe in You
I'll always believe in You
Though I can't see You with my eyes
Deep in my heart Your presence I find

Lord I believe in You
And I'll keep my trust in You
Let the whole world say what they may
No one can take this joy away

Lord I believe
Born from above
You are God's only chosen one
You're the one and only true way
To the Father's heart

You died for all sin
Then you rose and now live again
Conquering death and the grave
So that I might live

—Tommy Walker

*W*hy do I believe in Jesus? It's a reasonable question and at the heart of my witness. If someone comes up to me and challenges me to explain why, what do I say? After all, you can't see the Lord. He doesn't speak in an audible voice—not often anymore, anyway. He doesn't materialize in front of us or make objects move. He doesn't obey our commands, like a genie so that we see a direct cause and effect. Imagine saying to a friend, "You want to see why I believe God exists? Here, God, open that door. Blow that trumpet. Reveal Yourself to her so I don't have to keep talking about You. She'll just believe."

It's important for us to understand why we believe, not only because it's an essential part of our witness, but it helps when we have doubts. And believe me, I have doubts from time to time.

A while ago, at a moment when things weren't going all that well with a project I was working on (one I was sure the Lord wanted completed as much as I did), I began having doubts. And, in an effort to bolster my belief, I began to list all the proofs for the existence of God.

Yes, proofs. Scientists today can hardly wait to tell us that there is no proof for the existence of God, but proof is all around us.

I felt my desk. It exists. I can touch it. It has substance. And my desk is a proof that God exists. It's made of "stuff." In this case, wood. If God doesn't exist, where did anything come from? Did it just will itself into existence? And if it did, where did its will come from? The old philosophers used to call this "the first cause." And there's so much stuff that the first cause caused. Billions and billions of planets and more billions and billions of stars, and billions of tons of gas and tiny particles.

Even if you subscribe to the idea that all that "stuff" has always been here, you have to reason: "OK, *always* is a nice concept, but we're talking about stuff here—physical things—all those things have to come from someplace." In our imaginations we can see things just popping into existence, but *not* in reality. Even when we see a magician pulling a rabbit out of a hat, reality tells us the rabbit was somewhere else, just waiting to be revealed. Something from nothing is impossible—*without a Creator, that is*. And, in the case of my desk, we're talking about very *real* wood. The only way it could get here is if a Creator created it.

But just as feeling the reality of my desk shows me that there's a Creator, when I see the order, or laws, that typifies His creation, it tells me He is an *intelligent* Creator.

Following God's Order

Where would a farmer be if crops didn't obey laws? If he couldn't count on the seeds reacting in a certain way to fertilizers, moisture, and warmth? What if it took a month for corn to grow one time and a year the next? Corn always reacts the same.

And the chemicals all obey rules. They react the same to the same stimuli every time. If they didn't, how could manufacturers consistently make Saran Wrap or Styrofoam cups? Or even paper or ink? If chemicals reacted inconsistently to one another, how could gasoline be made to work the same way twice? How could food additives be kept from accidentally killing you?

What kind of world would this be if when iron was struck it crumbled one time and exploded the next?

Chemicals have no brain. They just obey. And where did the rules or the capacity to follow them come from if not from a Creator?

Chaos comes when order breaks down: witness Solomon's room before I clean it. Order does not come from chaos: witness when I ask Solomon to clean his room.

So that night when my doubts were working overtime, I wrote down these things. And I have to admit, it worked a little. The evidence of a Creator was substantial. Yet a discordant tune was still playing in my heart. Maybe it wasn't so much the existence of God that I doubted—maybe it was His love and my place in the plan for His kingdom.

About then I heard a whimper coming from Isabella's room. Sliding the chair back from my desk as silently as I could, I went down the hall and into her room. A blush of light from the hallway fell across her sleeping form. Her arm lay over the top of the covers and in the whisper of light I saw her little hand gripping a bit of blanket. This is the most precious of times for a mother, to stand over her sleeping child, seeing her chest rise and fall, her face so soft and innocent.

I knelt by her bed and slipped my finger into her hand. In her sleep, her tiny fingers closed around mine. Oh, my, her fingers were wonderful, so delicate, so perfectly formed, so innocent in all they had done. I thought of Psalm 139, how God formed us in the womb, how He knit us there, and how we are fearfully and wonderfully made. How could my elegant and beautiful Isabella be created by anyone but a loving Creator?

I prayed for my daughter as I knelt there. And for my son and my husband. And I knew as I prayed that I was in the throne room of the God who knew me from before the foundation of the world. My Lord Jesus. My Father. My blessed Holy Spirit.

I was so filled with the knowledge of Him. I went back to my desk and continued to work on songs for this album. A song came to mind that a friend had recently sung in church. I made a note to myself to call her and ask if she would send the lyrics. They were perfect—as though my very thoughts had been interpreted and conveyed through the song. And I say it again now without a hint of doubt, "Lord, I Believe in You."

Verses Behind the Song

Though you have not seen him, you love him; and even though you do not see him now, you believe in him and are filled with an inexpressible and glorious joy, for you are receiving the goal of your faith, the salvation of your souls. (1 Peter 1:8–9)

I absolutely love these verses. They sum it all up for me. The fact is, we can't see God, yet we believe. We see His hand at work in every area of our lives. As I have heard it said many times before, God is like the wind. We cannot actually see the wind, but we can certainly see its effect on all it touches. So it is with God. The moving of His hand is unmistakable. There are times, however, when we are faced with circumstances that are less than desirable and we question whether God has ordained them. It's at those very moments that we must ask ourselves, "What do I believe?" "What is my faith made of?"

In the face of frustration, what will your answer be?

What Do I Believe?

I believe God took the form of man and walked among us. I believe that man, Jesus, died on the cross. I believe I'm forgiven because of the blood He shed for me on that cross. I believe He rose from the dead on the third day. I believe He is coming again. I believe He's preparing a place in heaven for those of us whom He calls daughters and sons. I believe in the Bible. I believe it is the inspired Word of God.

Do you believe the Bible? Read it. It is filled with stories, parables, prophecy, and truth. The Bible is a history book too. It has withstood scrutiny and can stand with any other history book. But the catch is that we as Christians must believe the whole thing—in its entirety; nothing more, nothing less.

I've met people who pick and choose stories and truths from the Bible . . . and usually just the good ones—the ones that support their philosophy. That's the problem though. It is their philosophy, not God's. We are called to a higher standard than one of our own creation. We are called to holiness—something we cannot attain on our own. Something that requires faith.

More than just a history book, a storybook, or a book of moral truths, the Bible is the very breath of God. His very words written by the hands of willing men who possessed faith of an unwavering nature—not unlike the faith to which you and I are called. These men trusted that what God was asking them to do was real. I'm sure many people ridiculed and scorned them for entertaining such fantastical ideas. "Ha! Words inspired by God Himself? How could you fall for such foolishness?" they might say. Some believed and some didn't.

Have you ever tried to have a discussion about the Bible with someone who doesn't believe it? It's difficult. Really, you just hit a brick wall. You may attempt to argue your point using the Bible as your proof, but since they don't believe the Bible, you don't have any common ground upon which to get a foothold. What do you do? How can you vividly convey the compassion, kindness, love, and truth of God in this book unless you have a believing audience? First, you must realize that hitting a person over the head or strong-arming them with the Bible will only drive them farther from the truth. Second, you must realize that your life and how you live it is the best example of belief. If you truly believe what you say you do as a Christian, then that belief will reflect in your actions, words, attitudes, and relationships. Living what you believe is more convincing than words.

What Is My Faith Made Of?

I received a letter not long ago from a friend. She is one of those people who prefers the buffet style of religion, selecting this and that from here and there to make a brand of God and/or godliness to suit her lifestyle. (It goes without saying, although I'm going to say it anyway, that we are to adapt to God's standard, not the other way around.) She and I got to know each other rather well, having worked together several years ago, and I became very well acquainted with her life and her beliefs, and she knew who I was and whose I was.

We had lost contact with each other for some time when I received the letter from her. She closed it with a phrase that really caught my attention: "Crystal, I love what you're made of." We haven't spoken much since. I can only assume that something I said or did got her to thinking, and I wonder what she is thinking about. How many people see your faith being vividly and actively lived out?

The strangest thing about my friend's comment was that during the time when we were better friends, I was struggling spiritually. I was doubting, I was questioning, and I was frustrated, and yet my faith remained firm. That is in no way a credit to me. Far from it. I am fully aware that my faith relies solely on my dependence on God. Faith is made of what we can't see (see Heb. 11:1). Sometimes we can't see God's purpose for our lives or the circumstances involved, but we stand firm. That is faith.

ELEVEN

god and i

I have pride He is meek
I have shame He is glory
I'm deceitful He is truthful
I'm not worthy but He is the giver

His death for my life God and I
If apart from Him I know I would surely surely die
I know that I'm not much to give
It's only for His love that I have my life to live

He has fullness I am so empty
He is love I need so much love
He is always there I am always found
He is the giver I'm not worthy

—Brian Ray

he kids and I were visiting my mom and dad in Washington state while Brian stayed behind to work. Visiting my folks is always fun, especially for the kids. My mom is really into being a grandma. She's constantly making installments on their hearts by baking them cookies, or buying their favorite coloring books, or playing hide-and-seek, or doing a hundred other things.

Everything they want, they get. Plus my folks have a big house so the kids have plenty of room to run around.

Fortunately for me, Mom gets tired periodically and has to put the cookies and coloring books down, has to stop seeking whoever's hidden only God knows where, and sits down with me for a cup of tea. That's when she and I get reacquainted, which takes all of two seconds, then we're back to being our "wild and crazy" selves. My mom and I are nuts about each other. It's not a minute before we're laughing about this or that, catching up on family stories—of course, she wants to hear every endearing little thing the kids have had the nerve to do without her. And, although we have our little battles—some not so little—they always end with one of us calling the other, and in tears, apologizing. Then, with the storm cleared, we're back to *mama* and *daughter* talk.

Well, one of those battles happened on this trip.

As I said, Brian was home alone. And unlike Macaulay Culkin, he had had no intruders to battle, so after work Brian had nothing to do. He missed us. And when he misses us he usually does two things. He gets a little melancholy, and he writes lyrics to songs—usually reflecting his mood.

In this case, he began to think about his relationship with the Lord. First let me say, Brian has a sound relationship with Christ. He prays often and fervently—alone, with me, and with the kids. He reads the Bible faithfully and works hard to apply the precepts of Scripture to his life and our family. In everything he does, he tries to be a good Christian husband and father. And he maintains the highest moral and ethical standards in our business and ministry.

But even as good a Christian man as he is, when he compares himself—when any of us compare ourselves—to the purity of God and the absolute sinlessness of Jesus, a huge chasm opens up between them. It is like the difference between black and white. From this personal exploration came the song, "God and I."

We ascribe to the Lennon-McCartney school of collaboration. Each of us writes as we are inspired, then we share it with the other and invite comments. Having written the words, he wanted to share them with me. Invariably, what one of us creates needs to grow a little on the other one. The first impression is usually, "Well—okay—I bet it'll get there with just a little more work." Later we tend to come around.

That was my first reaction when I read Brian's fax.

My mistake was to voice it in front of my mom.

A consummate musician sensing she was needed, she immediately grabbed the page with one hand and a pen with the other. Then she uttered *the words:* "Well, let's see what we can do here to make this 'sing.'"

And she started editing Brian's song.

"What are you doing?"

"I'm making it better."

My jaw dropped squarely on the table, as I watched her scratch out a word, then another, then a whole line. Then her eyes squinted and the tip of her tongue poked from the corner of her mouth—she was thinking. A moment later replacement words poured from her pen.

"This is Brian's song," I said. It was an astonished protest. Neither Brian nor I would ever think of editing the other's work. We might say it needs work, or it doesn't seem to capture what you're trying to say, or you're working too hard to make it rhyme, or something like that. But we would never change a word—that's the original author's job—and if, and *only* if, that person agrees. We respect each other's work too much to change it without asking.

"Mom, you have to stop. Right now. You just have to."

"No, no, dear. You'll love this when we're done."

"We're done? We? Don't bring me into this."

"But you said yourself it needs a little something."

"But that's up to Brian to—"

"He'll thank us."

"There you go with that *us* again. Mom. Please. You really don't know what you're doing."

"Sure, I do. I've had training."

"But it's not your song."

"Are you saying I don't know music?"

That's the moment the fight began. My objections had become a personal attack.

Of course, after a couple of hours of fiery words and fuming—and after my dad got involved to put everything in perspective—the fight ended. Actually, my dad said something that became very important to both Mom and me.

The Importance of a Personal Relationship

Up to that point I understood the boundaries that Brian and I had drawn around our work, and I deeply respected them. But I wasn't completely sure why we had drawn them. In a way I'd always chalked it up to pride.

After all, we were writing songs to the Lord. Wouldn't we want those songs to be as good as possible? And aren't two heads sometimes better than one in the creative process—each person bouncing ideas off the other, making the created thing better? Isn't that how and why the Lennon-McCartney school of collaboration worked so well?

"No, it's not pride," my dad said, "Brian is writing about his relationship with Jesus, his God, his Creator—the one Person in the universe who knows him better than anyone and loves him. Not loves him *anyway*—but just *loves* him. That's a tremendously personal relationship and every word of a song like that is important and personal. That's why you and Brian need to be masters over your own songs. It's not because of pride, but because no matter what the song's subject might appear to be, the real subject is your relationship with Him. And again, no one can put words in your mouth concerning that."

It truly goes without saying that every original word of "God and I" stood, and my mom had a long talk with Brian, apologizing for what she'd done.

Like most of what we write, "God and I" really grew on me, particularly as I began to see it through what my dad said. These words came right from Brian's heart. They express a wonderful relationship between God and one of His children—in this case, the one I love. But more important, as the song became more and more a part of me, it also began to reflect the relationship between God and me, as well.

Verses Behind the Song

As the heavens are higher than the earth,
so are my ways higher than your ways
and my thoughts than your thoughts. (Isa. 55:9)

Albuquerque—a couple of years ago.

We were about to perform to a packed house. As we do before every performance, Brian and I and the other performers got together to pray. Our prayer was simple. We thanked the Lord for giving us the opportunity to minister to those in the audience, and we asked that we might glorify Him.

Now, all of us, when we pray, have some kind of answer in mind. If we're praying before a soccer game, we want the Lord to help us win. If we're praying before we teach, we're expecting the class to go well. Our hope before that show was that all the music would come out as we rehearsed; that the vocals would be free of mistakes, that all the electricity would keep flowing.

No glitches.

As it turned out, God wanted something else.

Things started fine. All the technicals worked well: the speakers, the instruments, the lighting. The vocals were right on. I remembered all the words and hit all the notes. We were on our way to another good show. But as I began the fourth song, my voice collapsed. Literally. Sound was coming out of my mouth one second and no sound was coming out the next.

That's not entirely true. I could talk, but not sing—or rather I *could* sing, but it sounded *really* ugly.

So. A packed house and no voice. What now? Think quick, Crystal.

Drying the tears that immediately formed, I began to talk. I told the audience the problem. They didn't riot. Then I began to talk about the Lord. What He meant to me. How He was in control of even things like this. I gave my testimony. I talked about salvation. The audience was still with me, but I could see they were getting a little restless. Music. We needed music. I called a bunch of young folks from the front row onto the stage and, with full backup, we sang one of my songs. Then I called some more up and we sang another. More people and another song. The audience was loving it. I talked some more. Then we had more people up. The music was exciting and all the voices were crammed with heart.

At the end of the evening I gave the invitation as I always do and more people came forward than had ever before. What a night! A lot of people were saved, and I learned some important things about my Lord.

We presume so much. So often we put together our grand plans, just knowing beyond any doubt that we know best. Oh, we pray about what we're going to do. Brian and I prayed a lot about that particular series of shows. We wanted God at the center of every one of them. But after that, even though we prayed before each show, our secret prayer was always: *Make this show like the last one. No surprises, Lord. We've worked incredibly hard here to make it a good show.*

That night God was letting us know that His ways aren't our ways and His thoughts aren't our thoughts—and His show doesn't necessarily have to be our show.

Afterward, Brian and I talked about that show's incredible success—success measured in the number of people who came forward—and we came to this conclusion. Our witness, yours and mine, is simply telling someone else what the Lord Jesus has done for us, how He's changed our lives, how His service is the only rewarding service, how believing in Him has never let us down. Any witness requires believability. Because my voice faltered and I was suddenly struggling on stage, I became very real to that audience. Everyone can identify with someone having trouble. And when they saw me starting to have fun with it all—and when that fun included their incredible help—I became *very* real to them. So when I spoke about Jesus, they believed me. I was suddenly a friend telling them something very important.

Brian was right when he wrote "God and I." The gulf between the purity of God and our own is a huge one. It probably stretches from one end of the universe to the other. And yet nothing in this life or the next is as important as our relationship with God. But how do we span that chasm? We don't, really. Jesus does. When we take Him as our Lord and Savior the chasm disappears and our relationship with our Lord begins. Suddenly we are reconciled to our Father in heaven, suddenly we have the Spirit of God dwelling in us, suddenly our lives are different. We now want to please God. We now work to learn about Him and to trust in Him. The greatest adventure of our lives—a never ending adventure—begins.

My dad is right too. Our relationship with our Savior is a very personal one. Defining it seems to fall outside the ability of words to describe.

There are times when I'm in church and I see something incredible in the faces of older men. I'm not sure why it's the men, but at my church it seems to be. The pastor will be speaking about the Lord and how He works in our lives when suddenly, on a few of the older male faces, I'll see the hint of a smile. A knowing, calm smile as if a memory were blooming somewhere off in time, then a tear, a speck glistening at the corner of their eyes. Then, as if I'm seeing a glass fill with water, I see them fill with what I can only imagine is the Holy Spirit, perceptibly yet indescribably. Sitting there in the pews they look so close to Him at that instant, so very close.

I marvel at it.

I've talked to one of them about it, but he's not able to put it into words very well, either. "It's about giving everything over to Him, I think," he says. "But it's also knowing He loves you. Really loves you. I'm seventy-three, and I've seen the Lord prove His love for me a lot of times. I took it for granted when I was younger. I don't anymore. And I'm not there yet. Sometimes the closer I get to Him the farther away He seems. I probably won't be close enough until He takes me home. He's such a wondrous God. And, oh, He's been so very good to me."

"But how do you develop a close relationship with the Lord?"

He thought a moment. "You've got to want it," he finally said. "You've got to really want it."

Then his eyes twinkled at me and he moved on to rejoin his family.

Of course—you have to want it. What kind of answer is that? But after I thought about it for a little while, I realized it was the only answer. We have to *want* a close relationship with the Lord. We have to want it so much, we're willing to give up ourselves in the process.

When I stepped on stage in Albuquerque, I was there to serve the Lord. But I was serving Him on my terms. Once He took my singing voice that night, I was suddenly there to serve Him on *His* terms. I was no longer able to rely on the tried and true, the stuff I could do backward and forward. I had to rely on Him completely, knowing that whatever I had taken pride in in the past was no good to me now. Only He was.

Your relationship with God is so personal. It's wrapped up in who you are, what you do, why you do it. And not just the surface things, but the real you, the real reasons you do things. Very personal stuff. Some of it is perhaps a little scary to you. But whatever your situation, I urge you, if you haven't already, to begin moving everything you are closer to the Lord through Jesus. How you do that is between you and the Father. I know it has to start with prayer and a true desire.

My relationship with Jesus still has a long way to go. Like my older church friend, I probably won't be satisfied with it until He takes me home. But I've seen glimpses of what being close to Him is like. Small peeks at His intimate presence. And I want so much more. I want Him close when I'm on stage for Him, or playing with and teaching the kids for Him, when I'm doing anything as performer, wife, and mother. No matter what I'm doing, I always want it to be *God and me.*

TWELVE

for such a time as this

I built my house here
'Long side this mountain
This rugged mountain that stands so tall
I've had a good life
Above the lowlands
It's more than I'd asked for
But less than I'd dreamed

I've often heard a voice call down to me
If you'd climb higher you'd find wondrous things to see
But the way is steep and a storm may come

For such a time as this
Isn't it much too great a risk
I've never flown from the edge of a cliff
Never walked on the water
But if I turn away
How will I know what I have missed

Have I waited all of my life
For such a time as this
I've been content to
Not ask those questions
That stir the rivers
That move the waves
The windless waters
Are so much more peaceful
They calm my spirit
In silent song

I've often wondered what's eluding me
The yearning meant to free me from complacency
But the way is steep and the storm may come

Sometimes the thrill of soaring
Has to begin
With the fear of falling

—Anne Barbour

*A*nne Barbour wrote this song, as well as "The Lion and the Lamb" on *Beauty for Ashes,* my previous album. She is a very talented lady. Since I'm always interested in the creative impulse, when we were previewing the song for *Gold,* I asked her what led her to write it. This is what she said: "There's a kind of self-fulfilling prophecy about this song. If I wasn't a Christian and didn't know that God is in control, I'd think it was just a little spooky.

"I had just finished reading the book of Esther. I try to read through the Bible every year, so I had read Esther many times before. But this time it seemed to touch me more deeply. Especially when Mordecai told Esther there was no way she could escape the coming slaughter of the Jews and that she should try to enlist the king's help to stop it. Then he goes on to say that perhaps she was placed in the palace by God *for such a time as this.*

"I began to think about that: the idea that our lives can be a series of appointments—that God makes the appointments for us, then prepares us for them, and finally places us where we can keep them. Esther, a Jew, won the beauty contest, which gave her unusual access to the king, which gave her the opportunity to intercede with the king on the Jews' behalf.

"All this, of course, makes me wonder, *What divine appointment sits out there on my horizon?*

"One of those appointments was writing this song. Inspired by what I found in Esther, I started putting words on paper. I put down a single line—four words—then for the next several hours I just stared at them. And the blank section of paper below them. Finally, unbelievably frustrated, I gave up.

"A couple of months later my husband started reading a

book. That in itself isn't unusual. He reads a lot. But this one was a western. He never reads westerns. But for some reason he was drawn to this one. It was about Billy the Kid, and some rich Christian who imported missionaries from the east to minister to the opening west.

"Well, where my husband works, there was this gentleman who really isn't very nice—kind of crude and gruff, difficult to speak to. As it turns out this guy was reading a book about the same thing. It gave my husband something to talk to him about. And the story about the missionaries gave him a chance to witness. That night, my husband told me reading that book was like the Lord preparing him to witness to that guy. He then remembered I'd tried to write a song about the subject and suggested I try again.

"I didn't want to. I remembered how hard I had struggled over it and didn't want to go through that again. But for my husband's sake I relented. This time, though, the words poured out of me. I couldn't write fast enough. Yet when it was finished, it was a different song. Oh, it said the same thing, but very differently. Before, I'd been focused on Esther. Now it became very personal—almost intimate. When I finished, I called you right away. The spooky part was that you had been thinking about the same thing."

Anne was right. I had been thinking about that very issue. But a few months ago, when she originally sat down to write the song, I hadn't been. Had she called then I probably would have suggested she try someone else. But now the song fit perfectly into what we were beginning to see as *Gold*'s emerging theme—the struggles of the Christian life, and the reasons behind them.

A United Front

But God's preparation for Anne's call was even more specific.

A few days before, my mother and I were having a phone conversation. "You know," she began toward the end of it, "if you and Brian hadn't gotten married, we wouldn't have Solomon and Isabella. I'm glad you didn't listen to us, dear."

When I hung up I got to thinking about what she'd said. Brian and I *had* struggled with the decision to get married, a struggle made even more difficult because my parents were against it. But Brian and I did get married, and it turned out to be the right decision. Not only are we very happy, and we do have Solomon and Isabella, but our marriage brought something very important to our music.

We see our music as a ministry—because it is. But we're also in the entertainment and music *business*. We experience the same pressures as any secular performer. And the same temptations, particularly those that come with a certain fame and often dealing with people who want to make money promoting the talent God has given a performer.

Because of that, this business is both volatile and uncertain. And since the stakes are incredibly high, the temptation for others to take advantage of youth and naïveté is equally high. Even though we're mostly dealing with Christians, once in a while you'd never know it.

As a married couple, Brian and I talk things over. And we make decisions about the ministry together. When one of us carelessly leaves the Lord out of the process, the other one doesn't. Since we always consider the other's viewpoint, we're less likely to take foolish risks, and because we always want to give the other the best advice, we think things through. The fact that we're a family as well as business partners, makes our ministry far less vulnerable to the world's inclinations and Satan's wiles.

So—I was thinking about all this when Anne called and previewed the song for us. I knew immediately that God and Anne had created her song *for such a time,* and an album, *as this.*

Verses Behind the Song

And who knows but that you have come to royal position for such a time as this? (Est. 4:14)

God is never mentioned in the book of Esther. Not once. It's the only book in the Bible where He is not. Yet it's hard to find a book in Scripture in which He is more evident. Not only did we see God work out His plan through His relationships with common people but also at the highest levels of governmental power.

And what was God doing?

He was protecting His people from the tyranny of a powerful man and, in the process, showing them that He was there for them. He not only enabled them to survive but strengthened their faith as well.

But there's another dimension to the book of Esther—*Esther herself.*

Created for Good Works

She was a young, beautiful Jewish woman literally plucked from obscurity through a beauty contest to become queen to Xerxes, the ruler of Persia—a powerful empire that stretched from India to the upper Nile region. Xerxes ruled from 486 to 465 B.C. For Esther, things changed rather quickly. One day she was like normal Jewish folks, her skin weathered by the sun and sleeping on an earthen mat. The next day people bowed to her as a queen, her skin treated with perfumed oils, smelling the rich odors of roasted meats and flowers wafting through the palace of Susa, and sleeping on silk sheets.

Imagine yourself suddenly thrown into that situation—not sure of the rules, not sure if your power was equal to the comfort you enjoyed, and worried that simply saying the wrong thing at the wrong time to the wrong person might jeopardize it all. And now there was so much to lose. Imagine Esther making such a difficult change and still maintaining her equilibrium. And all indications are that she maintained it quite well.

Now sincere Christians can differ on just how involved the Lord is in our lives, and I don't pretend to have all the answers. But if we are to believe God's Word, my life, your life, all Christian lives have elements to them that are called by our Lord "good works." These are our works that, when tested on that last day, won't burn as wood, hay, and straw, but remain as gold.

Take a second now to look back on your life. What are some of your good works? Maybe you led someone to Christ. Or maybe you taught a Sunday school class. Or you raised your children, or perhaps you still are, like I am. Be honest with yourself. We all know that the Lord is intimately involved in these good works, so we're certainly not taking all the credit, but, after all, they are tasks the Lord has given us to do.

I have a friend who does a newsletter at church. That work is going to end up gold. I have another friend who helps churches implement their computers. And sometimes he helps me. Now that's really going to turn into gold. Good works are all those things we take godly—and I stress godly—pride in. Maybe you're still young and the list is short. Or maybe you're my dad's age and have had a life like my dad and mom and the list is long.

If we're to believe Scripture, it doesn't matter so much whether the list is long or short. What matters is that we do what we were given to do. And we do it lovingly, humbly, giving all due credit to the Lord.

The other thing that seems to be true of a Christian's list of good works is that one good work seems to prepare us for the next.

Is that true of yours? If you teach Sunday school, did your success teaching a small class on a relatively simple subject prepare you to teach a larger class on a more complex one? That principle is certainly true of my friend who puts together computer systems for churches. He started by installing a single computer that did only one thing and now he's installing several computers that are doing all sorts of exotic things—from payrolls to answering the telephones. Or maybe it's not so easy to see the link between the works you've done. Maybe it's easier to see how you've developed certain capabilities and disciplines in one area that have ended up helping you in others.

That certainly was the case for Esther.

One could easily make the case that God did nothing to prepare her for life in the palace. How could fitting in with commoners possibly prepare one for the intrigue in a palace court? But I don't think that's true. Let's consider the qualities that set Esther apart: her beauty, her humility coupled with an obvious regal confidence, her gentleness in dealing with the king, her intelligence, her bravery, her sense of duty and loyalty, and finally and most important, her love for the Lord. All of these were instilled in her solely by God with the help of Mordecai, her earthly parent.

How about you? How has the Lord worked in your life? Can you look back and see the trail of preparation, followed by good works, followed by more preparation? After all, we're all works in progress. We have no way of knowing how we will be used in the future.

Just as Esther had no way of knowing how she would be used.

After she led that privileged life for a while, after viewing an exalted future from her cloud-high window, it must have been difficult to hear that the time had come to risk everything, including her life. The evil Haman had caused King Xerxes to condemn to death all the Jews in Persia. Considering the size and location of Persia, that was probably most of the Jewish remnant from Babylonian captivity. Only the king's edict could save them, and, because of her position and heritage, only Esther was there to broach the subject to the king. If the king reacted negatively to her unrequested appearance before him, she would lose her life. This was a high tightrope she was about to walk. Mordecai sensed her hesitation and strongly warned against it. After all, she was probably born for this very moment in Jewish history.

With our preparation for the task, comes the responsibility for performing that task. Each time I go on stage, I am obligated to give everything I have for Him. It's my contract with Him.

You *are* responsible for teaching that class, or raising those kids, or feeding the poor, or building that house in Mexico, or leading that choir, or singing that solo, or writing that Christian novel.

Esther was also responsible for what she was given to do. And she took that responsibility. She commanded a three-day fast for all the Jews in Susa, a three-day time of prayer and communion with the Lord. Then she went in to see the king.

As you go through trials, as you learn things and apply them, as you gain experience, as you live your life from day to day, keep in mind that one day you may look back and realize that what has gone before was preparation *for such a time as this.*

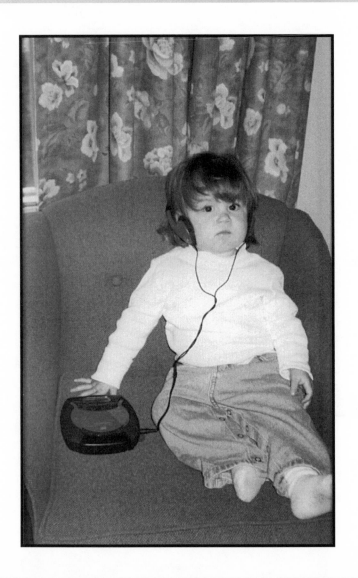

THIRTEEN

gold

Here's to the woman
Abandoned by her husband
Who left her for another woman

And to her children
For half the love they've been given
Has left them all of a sudden

Blessed are those who mourn
For they shall receive great comfort
But still I found death seems to bring forth
Life

All your heartaches
All your sufferings
All your trials
Are gold

Here's to the woman
Who's left to raise her children
She doesn't know the first thing about
How to make a living .

And all the birthdays and ball games
And Christmas mornings
Will never be the same

Blessed are the poor in spirit
For theirs is the kingdom of heaven
But still I've found death seems to bring forth
Life

All your sorrows
All your pain
All your trials
Are gold

—Chris Lizotte

*A*s I mentioned, my brother-in-law, Chris Lizotte, wrote this song. Married with children of his own, he knows the sacrifice two Christian parents make to assure their children the necessary physical, emotional, and spiritual nourishment. It takes two, he knows, as one parent relieves the other in a sort of relay to keep neither from getting too overwhelmed.

So when a dear friend's husband left her for another woman, abandoning both her and their three children, Chris was not only outraged at the husband, but devastated for that now dismembered family. "Gold" came out of his concern for that woman and her children.

Choosing "Gold" for this album, though, had its roots in my experiences and the experiences of some people I know, as well.

Tim and Jennifer went to a church I attended for a while. She was a nurse at a local hospital and he was a lieutenant in the Marine Corps and a helicopter pilot. They had no children. He was a handsome guy, she was lovely, and they were very happy. In fact, their happiness seemed invincible, as if it were walled and high on a hill, completely unassailable. But, of course, it wasn't. One night during a training exercise, while wearing experimental night goggles, Tim flew his helicopter into the side of a mountain. He and four others were killed.

A marine's wife is schooled in the idea that one day her man might not come home, but Jennifer wasn't prepared for this. There was no war, no bullets flying, no one lying in ambush for Tim. He had just gone to work that morning as usual and had not come home that night.

Naturally she was devastated. Yet after a while, her faith

kicked in. She went back to work and began treating those who were physically ill as she had before. But she was able to treat those who were spiritually ill with a powerful new weapon, a newly energized life witness.

Her colleagues would come up, offering sympathy that she graciously accepted, then they would marvel at how well she was doing. "It's hard, God knows, but I'm really comforted by knowing that Tim is in heaven with Jesus," she said. At least two of the other nurses were impressed enough with her composure to hear the rest of the gospel.

A couple of years after Tim's death, Jennifer began dating a man in the church who had been a confirmed bachelor and a spiritual underachiever, as he was quick to admit. They fell in love and now have two children. Soon after their marriage he became an elder in that church.

Did Tim have to die for all this to happen?

Well, not all of it. But Tim did pass on, as we all must, and through the testing that his death brought to others, gold emerged.

In affliction and adversity, how is it possible to see the positive pain? Jennifer knew she had to live one day, sometimes one minute, at a time. Her prayer, like all our prayers during such trials as these, was that she would have the strength to remain faithful to the Father, and that good might come through her faithfulness.

It's so difficult to imagine how good can possibly come

from certain events. Yet Scripture clearly teaches that it can, and will. After all, what possible good could have come out of Joseph being thrown into the cistern by his brothers, or Goliath humiliating the entire Israelite army, or the tragic stoning of Stephen, or the hanging of a lowly carpenter's son on a Judean cross? But growth did occur; and lives were changed. People were reformed in the heat of those afflictions, into something closer to the image of Jesus.

And nowhere is the heat as intense as it is for Christians in prison.

Faithfulness Becomes Gold

I have never been a prisoner. Even as a teenager, feeling the necessity to rebel every chance I got, I never felt that I was in prison (of course, that will come as a surprise to my dad!). In my quest to relate to prisoners, I've tried to imagine what it would be like. The only analogy I can come up with is that it has to be like being in hell: prison is a horrible place and there is no way out. There are no words you can utter, no apology you can make, nothing you can do that will set you free. Your only hope for freedom is to do your time—and your time feels like an eternity.

I am involved with a small prison ministry where periodically I sing and speak at the Sunday evening service. And no matter how often I go, it's an emotionally taxing experience that begins the moment I enter. Everything is so gray and stark, and though the prison personnel are friendly, they're as impersonal as the metal detectors and the iron gates. Then, each time I'm led to the prison courtyard, the same feeling sweeps over me: I have no idea what the women I am going to meet that night are going through, so how can I possibly relate to them or their situation?

They, on the other hand, know exactly how I'm living. I'm *free,* and as I arrive they watch me with steely eyes, wanting a piece of that freedom.

Standing there is also frightening. I'm sure that one day the guards will forget who I am and just not let me out. But standing there is also exhilarating. Going through all that security, I invariably experience the noble feeling of *impending good.* With so many souls in pain, it's easy to believe at least someone will be touched.

One particular night an overwhelming sense of inadequacy seemed to visit me with unusual intensity. What could I possibly say between my songs that *would* be meaningful? After all, I'm just a preacher's daughter whose life of ease couldn't possibly have prepared me to say anything of value to these inmates. As I stood there with my accompanist, something inside me was posing a very good question: *What in heaven's name am I doing here?*

Enter Laura. About forty-five, nice-looking, she had met us at the gate with Bruce, our sponsor. I figured she was a new member of the ministry team since I hadn't seen her before and because she spoke so fluidly about the women's excitement at our coming. During the service she was an inspiration—singing along, clapping, smiling. No one was more surprised than I when she walked us back to the exit gate, said her warm good-byes, and then remained behind bars as the door swung shut.

Less than a week later I got a letter from her. After expressing her gratitude for our visit, she shared some incredible insights into prison life and its reflection of the heart of God. Here is a brief excerpt from that letter:

> . . . You would be surprised at who God uses to touch those of us in here. Ministry teams come in that are composed of redeemed drug addicts, which of course, as they begin giving testimony, touches many. But then there are those in here who have come from the same exact background as yourself. I am one of them. I am a preacher's daughter. I have been in here for fifteen years. I will get out when God says go. So just know that God uses lots and lots of different people to bless us. Even you! You thought that you had nothing in common with any of us (besides the fact that we are all part of the same body of Christ) but you do. I can relate to you, and so can a lot of other girls in here. I am glad that you were obedient to the call of the Lord because you really blessed me and everyone else. Thank you . . .

Before I finished reading, tears were raining on the page. And I was crying for so many reasons. One was simple gratitude to my Lord for Laura's thoughtfulness. In spite of all my anxieties, I had been of value that night. I had taken the time to go and God had turned my faithfulness into gold. Sometimes our willingness to place ourselves in a difficult situation is all that's needed to begin the refining process.

Not long after receiving this letter, Brian and I began writing songs for this new, as yet untitled, album. But before I had written a single one, I heard Chris's recording of this song again. Its powerful message, coupled with the feelings Laura's letter had awakened, made "Gold" a must. Then, as songs presented themselves, they all seemed to crowd around "Gold"'s scriptural message. I pray it touches you as it has me.

Verses Behind the Song

"But he knows the way that I take; when he has tested me, I will come forth as gold." (Job 23:10)

Even though I'm well aware of God's promises, when hard times hit, immediately I think this is the time God will let me down (which, of course, He never has). Then, I cry out: *Why am I being put through this (whatever this happens to be)? If God wants to teach me something, why doesn't He just write me a note or enroll me in a seminar? Something at Lake Tahoe is always nice.*

The Refiner's Fire

Well, the note He writes me is His Word, the Bible. And He, like any teacher, knows that experience is the only true teacher. Yet teaching may not be the only thing He has in mind. He might have refining in mind, as well. When thinking how I might describe the refining process from God's perspective, I couldn't improve upon a piece of writing by Arthur T. Pierson:

> *Our father, who seeks to perfect His saints in Holiness,*
>   *knows the value of the refiner's fire.*
> *It is with the most precious metals that the assayer*
>   *takes the most pains,*
> *And subjects them to the hot fire, because such fires*
>   *melt the metal,*
> *And only the molten mass releases its alloy or takes*
>   *perfectly its new form in the mold.*
> *The old refiner never leaves his crucible, but sits down by it,*
> *Lest there should be one excessive degree of heat to*
>   *mar the metal.*
> *But as soon as he skims from the surface the last of the*
>   *dross, and sees his own face reflected, he puts out*
>   *the fire.*[2]

One of the impurities God, the Refiner, forces to the surface in my life is *worry*. And, believe me, He forces it to my surface quite often. Being in ministry, there are a million things to worry about: Is our music both contemporary and God-honoring? Are the lyrics both understandable and meaningful, yet evocative? And the granddaddy of all worries, will God continue to pay the bills through our ministry? But I'm also a wife and mother, and that responsibility brings with it another million worries, maybe even a few more than that.

Over the years I've seen a pattern to my worrying:

- I'm aware there's a problem.

- I invent the worse possible outcome to the problem.

- I see all the problems this new problem can cause.

- I see all the worse possible outcomes of all those new problems.

- I see how helpless I am to respond to all those new problems.

- Desperately, I come up with a plan of action to address the first problem.

- I stew about what happens if the plan of action doesn't work—or if I make mistakes while working on the plan.

- I stew some more, worrying that I may be addressing the wrong problem while the real problem goes unaddressed.

Do you get the picture? With me, worry tends to build on itself until I'm tied in emotional knots. Finally, when the knots are big and tight enough, I stop—and just take stock. Normally, the first thing I do is get out the biggest calculator I can find and count up my sins. A list of some of them might go like this: unbelief, being anxious, not seeking the Lord often enough in prayer, and not drawing upon those closest to me for help and strength.

Then I gird myself up and try to proceed without those sins. I pray every time I begin to worry. I talk whatever it is over with Brian, or anyone else who might have reasonable input. I force myself to believe the Lord isn't going to let me down, and I work at being calm. Then, as I continue, I watch for the Lord at work. As I see Him working, I note it in my journal, or in the Bible beside a particularly applicable verse, so that I can draw upon that experience later.

As often as I worry, you'd think I'd be getting the hang of *not worrying* by now. And, little by little, I am. I've seen the Lord work so often in my life, that the dross of those sins I've listed is being skimmed away bit by bit. And as it is, the gold that marked the purity of God's original creation is shining through more brilliantly. Slowly, I am being refined.

FOURTEEN

the gold of your faith

*T*he music has faded—maybe one or two of the songs linger on in your memory. Maybe a phrase or two, or perhaps just a word still clings to your consciousness, like a sunspot on the retina.

Maybe one of the songs touched you in a special way. Or maybe it was the whole experience of *Gold*.

Whatever the impression our effort has made on you, there are a few thoughts with which I'd like to leave you.

A Word of Encouragement

The first is a word of encouragement. As Job 23:10 says, "But he knows the way that I take; / when he has tested me, I shall come forth as gold."

As one of His people, He knows you. He knows you far better than you know yourself, knows every sin you've ever committed, knows every dark corner of your heart—and no matter what you're going through, no matter what issues you're dealing with, He's right there with you. But more than that, He loves you with an unfathomable love, a love that is working minute by minute in your life to make sure every step you take works together for your good. So, as you walk along your particular path, watch for Him.

A friend tells the story of driving through the California high desert. It was dusk with a moonless night coming, and he came upon a lady standing next to her car. She waved at him when his lights hit her and he could see her flat tire. Saying a little prayer for protection, he stopped and immediately saw three little heads poking over the backseat—obviously her children. Well, she didn't have a spare, and the tire on the car had been mangled pretty badly. She told him she was on a cross-country trip trying to get to a job in the San Francisco Bay area. She had enough money for food and lodging but not to replace a tire.

My friend is in the ministry and doesn't have much money. In fact, every nickel has a very specific place to go. But for whatever reason, he believed her and knew he had to help. Loading everyone in his car and throwing the mangled tire into the trunk, he headed for a nearby town. After spending nearly fifty dollars on a new tire, he returned to the woman's car. As he put the tire on, he was able to share the gospel of Jesus Christ with her. Then he said good-bye.

Before he had driven another mile, Satan started working

on him. It occurred to him that she was probably lying. He had spent a good portion of the rent money the Lord had provided—now he was testing the Lord by wanting Him to provide more. She was probably fleeing the law and he'd end up accused of being an accessory.

As the night dragged on, it became more and more difficult to keep from worrying. The next morning he awoke unrefreshed and went about weighed down with concern. After all, a major part of his witness was to show God's faithful provision—begging for money seemed pretty inconsistent with that.

But about ten that morning he got a call from a guy who sounded rather used to getting his own way. "I got a call from my daughter," he said. "You helped her. I'm going to wire you the money you spent—plus a couple of hundred more for your trouble."

"Really? But just the fifty's fine." My friend heaved a huge sigh of relief and felt his nearly empty reservoir of belief refilled.

"No. I owe you something extra."

"But you don't."

"My daughter hasn't spoken to me in four years. She hates me, maybe for good reason. The jury's still out on that. But you were so good to her, and what you said about God afterward mattered so much to her that she risked a call to me. She wanted you to get your money back. It was good talking to her. I love her, but I'm not that great at showing it. So God—Jesus—makes things better? Well, I guess the jury's out on that one too."

"No. In fact for those who love Jesus, there is no jury, no judge, just love and the Lord. You got a minute?"

So—as you walk along your particular path, watch for His acts of love and watch how He shows His love for others through you. There's no greater thrill than seeing His footsteps right alongside your own.

A Word About Your Gold

Recently Brian's grandmother, Gloria, went home to be with the Lord.

She was a fine Christian woman and we loved her dearly. She lingered in the hospital a few days, suffering from a brain tumor, so her death was not unexpected. Brian's mother was with her almost constantly during those last days. They were very close. As you know, both my parents are still alive, and I pray they'll live until the Lord returns. I wouldn't know what to do without them. So it's hard to for me to know what my mother-in-law was going through, watching her mother close in on death.

She knew that her mother was going to heaven—to be absent from the body is to be present with the Lord. She also knew that her mother was suffering no pain. The Lord was blessing her parting with a gentle calm. But still, this was her mother there in sterile white sheets, soon to take her last breath. This was the mother who had loved her for fifty years, had dressed her for school, had worried about her, shed tears for her, loved her as much as any human being could. She was as much a part of her as her own heart. Here lay the woman who had prayed her into the kingdom, who had wrestled with God on her behalf. She seemed untouchable—a detached entity—for the first time ever.

After sitting by her mother's side for most of the day, Brian's mother left to get a cup of coffee. When she returned, her mother had passed on. "She looked so different in death," she told us. "Before, even unconscious, she had the fire of life in her cheeks and her skin. But the fire was gone. She looked cold—like an empty hull, a body mask. And particularly her face—just chalk. I felt if I touched her, she'd crumble, for everything inside her that made her who she was, was gone. She was with Christ."

We inhabit our bodies for only the time we're here and then we go to be with Jesus. He tells us to store up our treasure where He is—where it won't rot or be stolen. So, as we're tested, as we struggle through our Christian lives as best we know how, we become more refined. What we leave behind is just chalk. What matters is what we have stored up there. Grandma Gloria stored up a whole bunch in heaven, and we are her proof, her certificates of deposit. For it was through her prayers that we were all touched, some of us with salvation, all of us by her intercession and her love.

So now as you turn off the album, or close this book, my hope for you is that you go on to touch others with your prayers and your actions. That when you follow Grandma Gloria to heaven, your account will be rich with your good works—rich with your *Gold*.

notes

Chapter 2

1. Spafford, Horatio G., "It Is Well With My Soul."

Chapter 13

2. Pierson, Arthur T., "Refiner's Fire," *Streams in the Desert,* (Grand Rapids, MI: Zondervan, 1997).

photo captions

Chapter 1

Solomon, Brian, and I enjoy a musical moment in 1994.

Chapter 2

I recorded the *Beauty for Ashes* album when I was pregnant with Isabella.

Chapter 3

My dad, the Reverend Hollard Lewis, in the atrium of Detroit First Nazarene Church in 1994.

Chapter 4

Brian and me on our wedding day, April 8, 1989.

Chapter 5

My school picture from my freshman year of high school, age 14.

Chapter 6

Solomon and Isabella rest on yet another hotel room bed.

Chapter 7

The Word of God is sharper than a two-edged sword.

Chapter 8

Start 'em early!

Chapter 9

Our family Christmas photograph, 1996.

Chapter 10

Brian and me, 1994.

Chapter 11

The cover photo for *The Lewis Ladies,* an album that featured myself and Mom and my sisters, Candace and Cassandra.

Chapter 12

Daddy (Brian) and Isabella, overworked.

Chapter 13

Isabella in a hotel room on tour . . . listening to Mommy?!

Chapter 14

Theatrical picture of Crystal.